A COMPLETE HISTORY OF
CALVARY
PRESBYTERIAN CHURCH
GRAND RIVER AND VICKSBURG AVENUES, DETROIT, MICHIGAN

FROM ITS BEGINNING IN 1868
UNTIL ITS 75th ANNIVERSARY
MAY 25th, 1943

WILLIAM DOWNIE, *Author*

INTRODUCTION

Part 1 is a brief History of Calvary Presbyterian Church, written in the year 1912 and covering only briefly the period from 1868 to 1912. The author was Robert McKinnell and the History was written to commemorate the 12th anniversary of Dr. Sutherland's pastorate on Michigan Avenue.

Part 2 immediately follows Part 1 and covers the 75 year period in detail from 1868 to 1943 by William Downie. The destruction of practically all of Calvary's records in storage by fire several years ago makes this history imperative.

BRIEF HISTORY OF THE CHURCH

PART I—THROUGH 1912
CALVARY PRESBYTERIAN CHURCH
HISTORICAL SKETCH BY ROBERT McKINNELL
OCTOBER 24, 1912

Early in the Spring of the year 1868, members of the Westminster Presbyterian Church and workers in some of the other city churches, realizing the need of a mission Sunday School in the western part of the city, held meetings in various neighborhoods in that section. The purpose in view was the location and establishing of a Mission.

Later, moving to a small frame cottage near the corner of Michigan avenue and Twenty-third street, the organization of the Calvary Presbyterian Sunday School was there effected May 25th, 1868, with Mr. Walter P. Kellogg as its first superintendent. Still later, the frame church building—located on the southeast corner of Maybury Grand avenue and Butternut street, was occupied by the Sunday School.

This was the nucleus of the Calvary Presbyterian Church, which was organized by a committee of Presbytery, October 3rd, 1872, the late Rev. Arthur T. Pierson, D.D., of the Fort Street Presbyterian Church, presiding. The Rev. William Aikman, D.D., of the Westminster Presbyterian Church, preached the sermon on the occasion. Articles of association were adopted November 18, 1872, and were recorded with the Clerk of Wayne County December 9, 1872, thus perfecting the complete organization fully committing the church and society to the Presbyterian form of government.

During the interval between the years 1868 and 1872, covering a period of nearly four and one-half years, preaching was maintained in the Mission by the late Rev. John G. Atterbury, D.D., and others; but it was not until the summer of 1872 that those worshipping in the Mission expressed a desire to be organized into a Presbyterian Church. At this meeting Mr. James Rankin was elected a ruling elder and served as the sole elder of the church until December 12, 1873. Later the session was increased by the election of Mr. Ebenezer Cheney and David Reid.

The members of the first Board of Trustees were: Darwin D. Davis, David S. Osborne, Samuel A. Plumer, John R. Gentle, Bradford Smith and Abel Shotwell.

Dr. Atterbury served as the first minister of the congregation, achieving results most acceptable. Under his faithful leadership, the young church made constant progress in that growing portion of the city. In July, 1874, Dr. Atterbury resigned and was succeeded by the Rev. William Grandy, who was invited to occupy the pulpit. Beginning his labors as stated supply August 1, 1874, he continued as such until December 8, 1878, when he resigned, much to the regret of the officers and members of the church and society.

In the year 1879 the congregation extended a call that was unanimous to that good and saintly man of God, the Rev. George W. Barlow, D.D., who was then the pastor of the Presbyterian church at Mason, Mich. This call was accepted, and on October 29, 1879, Dr. Barlow was installed pastor of the church. Under his pastorate during thirteen years, the church flourished continuously, experiencing two most precious and powerful revivals, God showing tokens of His favor by adding to the church large numbers who were brought to a saving knowledge of His grace.

The Sunday School, at this time, was one of the largest in the state, its attendance and membership being the highest in its history. With the growth of the church, there came the need of a new edifice. Dr. Barlow successfully stimulated the endeavors of the congregation toward securing a new site and in arranging for the erection of a new building; and the hearty co-operation and generous response of the members and adherents of the church, coupled with the interest and liberality of influential friends of other congregations, brought success. The new structure was completed and occupied for the first time in January, 1888. Dr. Barlow continued as the beloved pastor of the church until November 6th, 1892, when he was released to accept a call from the Presbyterian church at Lapeer, Mich. His pastorate was far reaching and covered a most important era in the history of the church; his influence and power were widely extended; his death in January, 1907, was greatly lamented.

Dr. Barlow was succeeded by the Rev. Andrew T. Wolff, D.D., who was called from the Presbyterian church of Frankfort, Ind., and was installed pastor February 19th, 1893. Dr. Wolff continued his labors with the congregation until December 31, 1894, when he resigned to accept a charge in one of our western synods. In May, 1905, Dr. Wolff's earthly labors being ended, God called him to his heavenly home.

In June, 1895, Rev. W. Hamill Shields, a graduate of Princeton seminary, was invited to supply the pulpit as temporary supply during the summer months. His faithful ministry won the esteem of the people, and in November, 1895, he was duly called to the pastorate. On December 13th, 1895, he was ordained to the gospel ministry and installed pastor of the church. Mr. Shields continued as pastor until July 22nd, 1900, when he resigned to accept a call to the church of Middletown, Ohio.

The sixth and present pastor is the Rev. David I. Sutherland, who was unanimously called from the Presbyterian church of Susquehanna, Pennsylvania, September 12, 1900. He was installed pastor October 25 of the same year. The church has never had a stronger and more forcible preacher. His faithful, earnest teachings and his watchful care, have been abundantly blessed. Constant accessions to the membership of the church and activities along all lines of work have marked his ministry. During his entire pastorate never has a communion passed without accessions to our membership. The church is numerically stronger today than ever before in her history, there being 665 communicants on the roll as reported to the last General Assembly. During Dr. Sutherland's ministry a considerable floating debt has been removed, the beautiful new pipe organ installed and other improvements made, the church having been but recently renovated and redecorated. Dr. Sutherland has made for himself a warm place in the hearts of his people, ever ready to respond to the many demands made upon him.

Because of changed local conditions in the parish and the many problems of the day to be solved, the demands on the pastor are becoming each year more arduous; however, with the co-operation of a united and harmonious people, aggressive work is being accomplished and the Kingdom of the Master advanced. We are sorry that space limitations set for this very brief sketch will not admit mention of the names of the worthy ruling elders, the sincere and able Sunday School superintendents, and the many other notable men and women connected with our earlier and present history. Many of these, whose lives were veritable benedictions, are not now among us, but we revere their memories. Let us now, in concluding this article, go forth in unity and harmony, firm in our faith and strong in our determination that the future years of Calvary shall be her best years. The officers of the church for the present year are:

Elders: John Munro, Robert McKinnell, William E. Selover, Walter E. Adams, William S. Mitchell, and Benjamin F. Matthews.

Trustees: Robert Lytle, John McKerchey, Warren E. Brinkerhoff, William H. Blackford, Fred G. Clark, Harry W. Harrison, Clarence Metcalf, Harry Mackie and Peter Grant.

Owing to the transitory condition of our parish, due to encroachments made by commercial and industrial enterprises and the secularization of the district to a greater or lesser degree—the personnel of our congregation changes every few years. Despite this fact, however, some of our present officials have been connected with the church for many years.

Elder Robert McKinnell, the stated clerk of session, although one of the youngest men in that body, is one of the senior elders of the church. He has been identified with the church for a longer period of time than has any of the present office bearers—his father moving to the locality nearly forty years ago and locating on Eighteenth street in 1873. The son's earliest recollections of attending the Sunday School extend backward to the autumn of 1877, during the ministry of the Rev. William Grandy. Growing up with the church, he has been intimately associated with her life, her history and her interests, to the present time.

Elder John Munro, the senior elder of the session, from the point of both age and service, has been connected with the church for the next longest period of time. Elder John Munro united with our church in 1881 by letter from the Knox Presbyterian Church, of Ingersoll, Ontario. He was made an Elder in 1887 and has been re-elected invariably at the close of each succeeding triennial term.

Elder William E. Selover has been identified with the church for over 25 years, uniting with us in July, 1887, coming by letter from the Second Presbyterian Church of Auburn, New York.

Elders Adams, Mitchell and Matthews were elected to the eldership during the past decade in the order named, becoming actively engaged in the work of the church during the present pastorate. Like their brethren, they have always displayed an interest in the "things of Zion," and in the words of Scripture, they have proven themselves to be "Elders that rule well." Of the members of the Board of Trustees, Mr. Warren E. Brinkerhoff, the every efficient treasurer of the church, has been associated with the church since the fall of 1884, (but not a member for all that time). Mr. Robert Lytle since 1889, and Mr. John M. McKerchey since 1895, and they have been active and valuable factors in the progress of our organization.

The remaining members of the Board, Messers. William H. Blackford, Fred G. Clark, Harry W. Harrison, Clarence Metcalf, Peter Grant and Harry Mackie date their connection with the church during Mr. Sutherland's ministry. Their relation in an official way has done much to bring the church to its present efficiency.

Mr. Mackie, our youngest trustee, has been connected with the church since childhood.

OUR ANNIVERSARY

Looking back over the years, would you have had them different? Many of us would answer "Yes," and yet, after all, how rich they have been in experience, in friendship and in opportunity, and at our very door today the privileges of the past stand out with amazing distinctness, for the past years have nothing in the way of noble service that the present does not bring to each one of us.

Calvary's past is rich to those who know it—rich in memories.

Can you look back for nearly forty-five years (since organization of Sunday School) of Calvary's history? Then you know those who labored earnestly and gave generously that this work might be formed on broad lines. Those of the present can now see the wisdom of its founders in locating a church in our community which has been a force for righteousness. No wonder we say, "God bless the memory of all who performed loyal service to Calvary."

This anniversary is no crisis in Calvary's history—it is just the time when we take a look backward, but a longer look ahead. Let us thank God for the past; for the tranquility and harmony which has been ours. Our only need now is stout hearts and sterling courage for the good days that are to come; for the past, rich as it has been, is of no value unless it helps us to build for the future.

CALVARY'S SEVENTY-FIVE YEARS

Let us thank God and go forward full of expectancy for the future work and advancement of the church, that it may be more influential and powerful in the years to come than in past years. Let us be patient in tribulation, fervent in spirit, ever serving the Lord.

ROBERT McKINNELL.

This concludes Part I, Robert McKinnell's sketch delivered October 24th, 1912 on the occasion of the 12th anniversary of the pastorate of Rev. D. I. Sutherland, D.D., in the Michigan Avenue church, razed in the year 1916.

MICHIGAN AVE. CHURCH

BUTTERNUT STREET CHURCH
at Maybury Grand

FOREWORD—PART 2

On October 24th, 1912, the twelfth anniversary of Dr. David I. Sutherland's pastorate was observed in the old church at Michigan and Maybury avenues. For that event Robert McKinnell wrote a brief historical sketch of the church from its beginning up to that date, which immediately precedes this Foreword. To the above occasion the writer and his wife were invited guests. Mrs. Downie's family were charter members of Calvary from the start in the year 1868 and her father, David Reid, was one of the first elders, his name still appearing in the articles of association of Calvary Church on file in the Wayne County Clerk's office, a copy of which appears in this history. Some time after the Michigan avenue church was built, Mrs. Downie's family moved into a new home on Third avenue, too remote for the transportation facilities of that day for them to continue their connection with Calvary, so part of the family, those living on Third avenue, brought their letters to the Second Avenue Presbyterian Church of which the writer was then a member. In due course of time Nellie F. Reid became Mrs. William Downie. Then in the year 1914 we moved to our present home. This was the year that Calvary started negotiations for the present site just a block away from our present abode, and of course Mrs. Downie rejoined Calvary and the writer also brought his letter.

Now Robert McKinnell, who recently entered his final reward, was a long-time faithful and devoted member of Calvary Church and the brief historical sketch that he wrote for the 12th anniversary of Dr. Sutherland's pastorate was absolutely authentic. However for the 64th anniversary of Calvary Church, held June 12th, 1932, twenty years later, a history up to that date was desired, including any and all historic events pertaining to Calvary that could further be unearthed. To this task the present writer was assigned and since 1932 has been compiling a scrapbook, from which, together with the 1932 edition, we now present a complete story of Calvary Church from the years 1868 to 1943, its seventy-fifth anniversary. The writer is presenting this in two parts:

Part 1 is a copy of Robert McKinnell's brief sketch from the year 1868 through 1912.

Part 2 in general is the substance of the present writer's history of the church from 1868 through the year 1932 as written in the latter year, including much additional matter of historic interest which the writer has gathered in the last eleven years and preserved in the scrapbook above mentioned, as well as a complete review of Dr. Bechtel's pastorate up to date. Every statement is authentic within the knowledge of the writer, reliable witnesses or taken from reliable records.

WILLIAM DOWNIE.

Author's Note: For complete details of dedicatory service of the frame Butternut Street church December 12th, 1869, see scrapbook in safe, page 30 or copy of Detroit Post, December 13th 1869.

For laying of cornerstone of the church at Michigan and Maybury avenues, see scrapbook in church safe, page 32 or copy of Detroit Free Press, May 31st, 1887.

For dedication of Michigan Avenue church see scrapbook in church safe, page 30 or Detroit Free Press January 26th, 1888. Any librarian in the Burton Historical Library, third floor of the main library, will refer you to these particular copies of these daily papers. The above newspaper accounts are all printed in this history later on, however.

The First Cottage Mission Of Calvary — Michigan Ave., near 23d —
The Artist's Conception — Drawn from description given by four persons in 1933 — who attended this Cottage Mission in 1868 —

Sketched by Dorothy Lee Beals.

To my old pastor, neighbor, friend
Dr. David I. Sutherland, D.D., and Mrs. Sutherland,
also their worthy successors,
Dr. Leslie A. Bechtel and Mrs. Bechtel
carrying forward the torch, I lovingly dedicate this
Story of Calvary Church.

WILLIAM DOWNIE, Author

"Through the deep caves of thought I hear a voice
    that sings:
Build thee more stately mansions, O my soul,
    As the swift seasons roll!
    Leave thy low-vaulted past!
Let each new temple, nobler than the last,
Shut thee from heaven with a dome more vast,
    Till thou at length art free
Leaving thine outgrown shell by life's unresting
    sea."

        —*Oliver Wendell Holmes.*

ALL OF THE PASTORS OF CALVARY CHURCH

REV. JOHN G. ATTERBURY, D.D.
1872-1874

REV. WILLIAM GRANDY
1874-1878

D. I. SUTHERLAND, D.D.
1900-1930

Present Pastor
REV. LESLIE A. BECHTEL, D.D.
Installed April 23rd, 1931

REV. GEORGE W. BARLOW, D.D.
1879-1892

REV. W. HAMILL SHIELDS
1895-1900

REV. ANDREW T. WOLFF, D.D.
1893-1894

THE MINISTERS' WIVES

MRS. JOHN G. ATTERBURY
1872-1874

MRS. WM. GRANDY
1874-1878

MRS. D. I. SUTHERLAND
1900-1930

MRS. L. A. BECHTEL
1931—

MRS. GEO. W. BARLOW
1879-1892

MRS. W. HAMILL SHIELDS
1895-1900

MRS. ANDREW T. WOLFF
1893-1894

THREE FIRST ELDERS

JAMES RANKIN

EBENEZER CHENEY

DAVID REID

FIRST TWO SUNDAY SCHOOL SUPERINTENDENTS

1ST SUPT.
WALTER P. KELLOGG

2ND SUPT.
H. KIRKE WHITE

(Most of the writer's 1932 history is included in the following pages.)

WHO WERE THESE EARLY WORKERS, THE PIONEERS?

Dr. John Guest Atterbury, D.D., the first pastor, James Rankin, the first elder, Ebenezer Cheney and David Reid, also early elders, Walter P. Kellogg, the first superintendent of the Sunday School, H. Kirke White, the second superintendent, and Rev. William Grandy, the second pastor. And the first trustees, Darwin D. Davis, David S. Osborne, Samuel A. Plumer, John R. Gentle, Bradford Smith and Abel Shotwell. What did they look like, and how did they act? What were their educational backgrounds and their traits of character? Whence did they come and where did they go? I will answer these questions insofar as I am able. But be it remembered that Calvary had a disastrous fire (described later) in which practically all pictures, all records and all data were destroyed and to reunite them again has been a Herculean task of several years' work.

FIRST BOARD OF TRUSTEES
SIX MEMBERS

SAMUEL A. PLUMER   DAVID S. OSBORNE   ABEL SHOTWELL

BRADFORD SMITH   JOHN R. GENTLE   DARWIN D. DAVIS

REV. JOHN GUEST ATTERBURY, D.D.

Was born Feb. 11, 1811, at Baltimore, and while a boy moved with his family to New Jersey. In 1831 he graduated from Yale College with honors and went to New York, where he was admitted to the bar. It was in 1836 that he came to Detroit and formed a law partnership with Samuel Pitts. The latter soon after went into the lumber business, and Mr. Atterbury continued his professional career as a partner of Alpheus Williams. In 1840 he married Miss Catherine Larned, and two years later, on account of the law business not being to his liking, he studied theology under the late George Duffield and also at Yale and Union colleges, and became a Presbyterian minister. His first charge was at Flint, Michigan, and after five years there he went to New Albany, Indiana, where he occupied a pulpit for 15 years. From New Albany he went to N. Y. and there served as secretary to the Board of Education of the new school Presbyterian Church, a position that he held as long as it was maintained. He then came back to Detroit to make his home, and has since done noble work in his chosen field.

He was a man of admirable qualities, a finished scholar and a gentleman whose gifts of mind and heart gave him wide influence. Mr. Atterbury had 12 children, of whom four sons and one daughter survive. At his death, August 24th, 1887, the funeral was from his late residence, 40 Edmond Place, Detroit, which was his home for many years. He was 76 years of age.

The above are extracts from articles in the Detroit News and Detroit Journal, August 25, 1887, the day following his death.

Referring to the Michigan Pioneer and Historical Collections, Vol. XIII, Page 288, we find that Judge Goodwin of the Michigan Supreme Court had died on the same day, and the Michigan Bar was called in session to honor the memory of Judge Goodwin. Judge Brown of the Michigan Supreme Court, presiding, made mention of the fact that Rev. Atterbury had preceded him by only a few hours on the same day.

On Page 545 of Vol. XIII, we find as follows:

A delegation from a Detroit military organization was invited by the mayor of Buffalo to visit that city. The writer says: "The invitation was joyously accepted, and the whole command, numbering 119 muskets, borne by the soldiers, some 19 or 20 of whom were distinguished young lawyers, among whom two were remembered especially, the Rev. Jack Atterbury, then a mad wag, a fellow of infinite jest, etc." This organization was the famous Brady Guards.

Volume 1, Page 428, he was elected December 3, 1842, secretary of the First Presbyterian Church, State and Farmer streets, now the site of the present J. L. Hudson Company store. It was then that he started the study of theology under Dr. George Duffield.

Vol. III, Page 438, tells of his taking over a church in Flint. Preceding him was Orson Parker. Quoting: "Parker, the first regular pastor of the church, was quite an effective evangelist in his day, but withal eccentric and many amusing stories are told about him. It is said that the society engaged him, as they supposed, for a year at a stipulated salary, but he construed the contract as calling for a stipulated number of sermons, and by getting up revivals and preaching daily, he managed to get in his whole year's work in a few months, and demanded his salary just the same as though his

104 discourses had been evenly divided through the whole 52 Sundays.

Failing to collect a church subscription from a delinquent brother, he would write a business note to his attorney, closing about like this: "Levy on his household goods, and if he doesn't pay, throw him and them into the street. Yours in Christ, O. Parker."

Volume VII, Page 404, we find Dec. 17, 1847, Dr. Atterbury organized the First Presbyterian Church at Lansing, with four members.

Volume V, Page 318, states that he declined a pastorate at Battle Creek church in 1866, at two thousand dollars per year salary.

Volume XII, Page 364, relates that between 1836 and 1841 he was president of the Young Men's Society of Detroit. Another officer on the board with him was Zachariah Chandler, the great Civil War senator from Michigan.

Now the question arises, was this man, Rev. John G. Atterbury, that I have been describing the same Rev. Atterbury that was the first stated supply pastor of Calvary Presbyterian Church? We naturally believe he was, because there is no minister of any denomination shown in the city directory by the name of Rev. John G. Atterbury except the man I have above described, but if you have any lingering doubt, the following extract copied from the Detroit Free Press files of August 25th, 1887, will dispel it:

"When Mr. Atterbury left New Albany, it was to assume the office of Secretary of the Board of Education of the New School Presbyterian Church at New York, and he continued to hold that position until it was abolished on account of the union of the two portions of the Presbyterian Church. He then moved to this city, and during his residence here has taken charge of Calvary Mission, and also having acted as supply when required by the absence of the pastors of the churches of this city and vicinity, etc."

Also, after tracing the name of Atterbury over a period of about 62 years in the city directory, I wrote General W. W. Atterbury, Philadelphia, president of the Pennsylvania Railroad, upon the advice of Mrs. H. N. Atterbury, since deceased, No. 2 Beverly Road, Grosse Pointe, who was a daughter-in-law of our own Dr. John Guest Atterbury, and I here reproduce General W. W. Atterbury's reply to my letter.

Broad Street Building
1617 Pennsylvania Boulevard
Philadelphia, May 13, 1932.
Mr. William Downie,
4447 Vancouver Avenue,
Detroit, Mich.

My dear Sir:

I duly received your letters on May 9, making inquiry concerning my father, Rev. John G. Atterbury and his connection with Calvary Presbyterian Church of Detroit, and now am glad to learn from your later communication of May 11 that much of the material you sought has been found in the Michigan Pioneer and Historical Collections in the Detroit Public Library.

What I give below may be of service, either in corroborating the data already in hand or furnishing additional items of interest.

A native of Baltimore, Md., where he was born in 1811, my father removed while an infant with his parents to Newark, N.J., during the War of 1812. After completing his education at Yale, father went to New York City to study law and was admitted to the bar. In 1836 he fell into poor health and went to Michigan on a double mission of business and recuperation. His health improved, he went back to New York, but returned to Detroit for the individual practice of law on Jefferson street, later joining first with Samuel Pitts and afterwards with Alpheus S. Williams. In January, 1843, my father resigned his law practice to prepare himself for the Christian ministry, going first to Yale Theological College and then to Union College. His first charge was the First Presbyterian church at Flint, Michigan, and his next was at New Albany, Indiana, where he was minister from 1850 to 1865.

My mother was Catherine J. Larned, daughter of General Charles Larned, who was Attorney General for the Territory of Michigan under Governor Cass, and who died in Detroit in 1834. Mother was born in Detroit, was married in 1840, and died in 1907. It was at New Albany, Indiana, that I was born in 1866.

Father's health again failing him, he recuperated in Detroit for a year and was then appointed secretary of the New School Branch of the Presbyterian Board of Christian Education at New York, and moved there in 1868, where he remained until 1871. He then returned to Detroit, where he aided in organizing the Calvary Mission and Church Congregation, and a record I have indicated that he was its pastor for three years. Another record states that John Guest Atterbury, D.D., of the Presbytery of Detroit, was Moderator of Michigan Synod over its meeting at Grand Rapids in 1873. Father was secretary of the Presbyterian Alliance of Detroit from its organization in 1872 until his death on August 24, 1887.

We regularly attended the Fort Street Presbyterian Church in Detroit, under Dr. Arthur T. Pierson, but father continued interested in Calvary Church for a number of years, or as long as his health permitted, which I should judge, was about four or five years.

I will have a copy made of a photograph I have of my father and will send it to you with a great deal of pleasure.

And I should be glad to have an opportunity to see the use that will have been made of the material you have gathered concerning old Calvary Church and father's early connection with it.

Very truly yours,

(Signed)   W. W. ATTERBURY.

Note: In the year 1882 about sixty years ago the writer heard Dr. A. T. Pierson deliver his farewell sermon in the present Fort Street Presbyterian Church, corner of Fort and Third street.

Knowing now that Dr. Atterbury lived and died at 40 Edmond Place (by the old system of numbering), I found at the city engineer's office that the new number on this house would be 84. I located the house, and the old No. 40 still remained painted on the glass over the door. The question now arose—was this house that I visited the one in which Dr. Atterbury lived, or might it not have been built after Dr. Atterbury's death. Consequently Dr. Bechtel went down and took a snapshot of it. This picture I sent to General Atterbury for verification, and received the following reply:

Broad Street Station Building,
1617 Pennsylvania Boulevard
Philadelphia, May 21, 1932.

Mr. William Downie,
4447 Vancouver Avenue,
Detroit, Michigan.

My dear Sir:

I am returning, herewith, the photograph received with your letter of May 19.

The house at 40 Edmond Place is the one in which my father

died in 1887. Originally it was a large single house, but after father's death it was made into a double house, one-half of which was occupied by my mother. Unfortunately, it does not appear that I shall be able to be present with you on Founders' Night, but let me renew my very best wishes for the complete success of the celebration on June 12.

Very truly yours,

(Signed)   W. W. ATTERBURY.

Note: A picture of the house is in the scrapbook which is in the church safe.)

I received also the following letter from General Atterbury:

Broad Street Station Building
1617 Pennsylvania Building
Philadelphia, May 20, 1932.

Mr. William Downie,
4447 Vancouver Ave.,
Detroit, Mich.

My dear Sir:

Here is a copy of photograph of my father, Rev. John G. Atterbury, D.D., which I promised to send you in my letter of May 13.

With all good wishes for the success of your Founders' Night celebration on June 12, I am

Yours very truly,

(Signed)   W. W. ATTERBURY.

Mrs. Agnes Telford Boothroyd, 2106 20th street, tells me of a certain Sunday when there was a large snow storm and no street cars running, Dr. Atterbury walked from downtown out to Calvary Church to conduct the services. According to Mrs. Boothroyd, his services were gratuitous. It is stated in this book opposite the picture of Dr. Atterbury that he was pastor from 1872 to 1874, but it is understood that he also preached prior to the year 1872 in the mission. The mission was incorporated into the church in 1872.

And so on Sunday, June 12th, 1932 there came the following telegram to the congregation of Calvary Church from the president of the Pennsylvania Railroad, the son of Rev. John G. Atterbury, D.D.

"Although I cannot personally greet you it is a pleasure to me to do so in this way upon the occasion of your second annual Founders' Day. Arranged in observance of the sixty-fourth anniversary of Calvary Church the opportunity is one I particularly welcome because of the association of my father with the early history of the church as one of its organizers and its first pastor, it is a joy to contemplate the growth of the work he helped begin. I want to heartily congratulate you and to express the hope that your future, meriting the guidance of the great Head of the Church may ever be increasingly fruitful." (Note: 64th anniversary of the Sunday School established 1868.)

WILLIAM WALLACE ATTERBURY.

(Note: Mr. Atterbury has since died.)

You will note that the above telegram came at the Sunday meeting of the 64th anniversary of the church during Dr. Bechtel's pastorate.

The following extract was taken from Page 24, Vol. 2 of Winder's memories, scrapbook of Fried Palmer, Burton Historical Library.

"One of them took to lumbering and the other to preaching. Pitts and Atterbury were a well known Detroit law firm in the 30's and 40's. Both members of the firm were excellent lawyers and their success in the legal line seemed to be assured when circumstances threw them into other occupations, in which they were both successful. John G. Atterbury was a man of small stature, slight physique, being about five feet five inches tall and weighing about 125 pounds. His face was striking and interesting and betokened a serious mood and practical intellect. His forehead was very high and broad with light blue eyes, acquiline nose and thin lips denoting decision of character. In 1871 he returned to Detroit where he organized the Calvary Church congregation and became its pastor in 1872."

Extract from Detroit Free Press of Sunday, Dec. 4, 1892:

"Sixty years ago, there was but one court in Detroit but the bar was remarkable for the number of illustrious members it contained, among the more eminent may be mentioned John G. Atterbury."

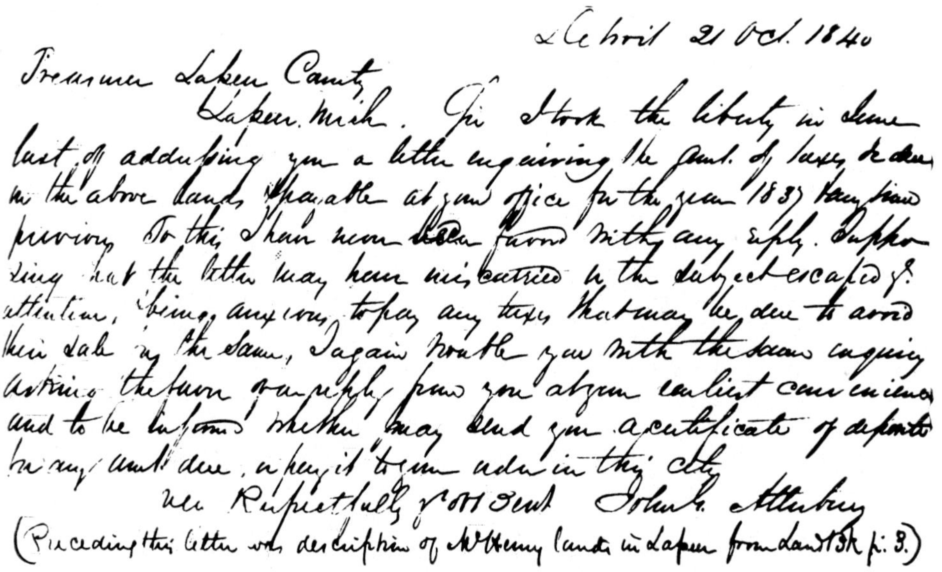

[handwritten letter reproduced in print below]

Photostatic copy of one of John G. Atterbury's letters in his own handwriting nearly 100 years ago. Below is a printed copy of the above cut.

Detroit 21 Oct. 1840.

Treasurer Lapeer County.

Lapeer, Mich. Sir—I took the liberty in June last of addressing you a letter enquiring the amount of taxes due on the above lands and payable at your office for the year 1837 and any time previous. To this I have never been favored with any reply. Supposing that the letter may have been miscarried and the subject escaped your attention, and being anxious to pay any taxes that may be due to avoid their sale for the same, I again trouble you with the same enquiry asking the favor of a reply from you at your earliest convenience and to be informed whether I may send you a certificate of deposit for any amount due and pay it to your order in this city.

Very Respectfully   John G. Atterbury

(Preceding this letter was description of McHenry lands in Lapeer from Land Book, page 3.)

Next time you visit Belle Isle go down Central Avenue and view the gorgeous, equestrian, mounted statue of Samuel Pitts, noted soldier, editor, lawyer and business man who over one hundred years ago was the law partner of our own John G. Atterbury, the first pastor of Calvary Church.

The following interesting and valuable historical record was given to the church by a friend in the Jefferson Avenue Presbyterian Church Feb. 6, 1908:

"Detroit, March 19, 1873. The Calvary Presbyterian Church, on Maybury Grand Avenue, near Michigan Avenue, in the western part of the city of Detroit, now under the care of the Rev. John G. Atterbury, has a fair congregation of families, in very moderate pecuniary circumstances, with a church property valued at about $6,000, with a debt of $1,500, which is pressing them sorely. The several Presbyterian churches of the city, after a full investigation by a committee of ministers and elders, have determined to aid, and the Fort Street Presbyterian Church is asked for $800, the First Presbyterian Church for $400 and the Jefferson Avenue Church for $300."

At the bottom of the document is a list of names of members of the Jefferson Avenue Church, with the amount of their pledges, totalling $300.

It will be noted in the old days Maybury was often spelled Mayberry.

I here introduce the following extracts taken from "The Metropolis of Michigan or Detroit," published by our familiar historian, Silas Farmer. They were secured and handed to me by our pastor, Dr. Bechtel.

FIRST PROTESTANTS IN DETROIT

"Protestantism entered Detroit with the English soldiers who came in 1760. The first Protestant missionaries were the Moravians. In April, 1782, four were brought here under arrest, accused of aiding in the American Revolution. They were acquitted of the charges, and on their release took up residence a small distance from the Fort and began their work of evangelization. However, in 1786, owing to persecution and continued opposition, they were compelled to leave.

"The first successful and continuous settlement and organization of Protestant work was that of the Methodists, who in the fall of 1810 organized the first Methodist Episcopal Church, with seven members. This church was disrupted by the War of 1812. After the war when Detroit was recovered by the Americans, the original seven were found here, still loyal and faithful to their profession."

FIRST PRESBYTERIANS IN DETROIT

"January 23, 1825, the First Protestant Society was organized into a Presbyterian Church, with 12 male and 37 female members. The Reverend Noah M. Wells was the first minister, taking up his work in May, 1825. Their property and first church were on Woodward Avenue, formerly the site of the English burying ground, including all of the block west of the alley between Woodward and Bates Street."

ORDER OF OLDEST PRESBYTERIAN CHURCHES

"CALVARY is the sixth in order of the Presbyterian churches organized in Detroit with a continued existence. The second was Westminster, organized October 6, 1837. Next in order came the Scotch or Central Church, November 10, 1843; Fort Street, February 21, 1849; Jefferson Avenue, February 8, 1854, and then Calvary Presbyterian."

CALVARY PRESBYTERIAN CHURCH

"This church is the outgrowth of a mission Sunday School, started in May, 1868, in a small building on Harrison Avenue which had been a grocery. Quickly it was moved to a cottage on Michigan Avenue, near the toll-gate. In the summer of 1869 a lot was donated by Bradford Smith, on the southeast corner of Maybury Avenue and Butternut Street, and a frame building, 36x75 feet, was erected at a cost of $3,500. It was dedicated December 13, 1869.

"October 3, 1872, a church was organized and incorporated with 16 members. The Reverend Dr. J. G. Atterbury, the first pastor, served until August, 1874. He was succeeded by the Reverend William Grandy as stated supply. On November 24, 1878, Mr. Grandy resigned, and on October 29, 1879, the Reverend G. W. Barlow was installed.

"The church seats 300. The average morning attendance in 1880 was 200. The number of members was 115. The pastor's salary was $1,400, and the total expense $1,800."

The above facts taken from "The Metropolis of Michigan or Detroit."

WHO WAS JAMES RANKIN, THE FIRST ELDER

My father owned and operated a grocery store at Fort and Eighteenth streets when I was a boy. Next door to the grocery store was our home. The two were one building, and over both was a large attic. In that attic were eight or ten barrels of brass goods, oak belting and articles belonging to a brass foundry. There was also a compass setting in a box and a fireman's hat, such as is used at fires. Those goods were stored there by a man whose name was James Rankin, a brass founder, who in 1868 rented from my father a house at 366 Baker street, now Bagley avenue, corner of Seventeenth street, and whose place of business was 91 Eighteenth street. In 1861 he lived and owned property at 157 Park street, and owned a shop at Congress and Third streets. He moved from 366 Baker street to 198 Eighteenth street in 1872. And about 1874 he left Detroit. Mr. Rankin never returned to get those stored goods. They had little value. I presume my father knew where Mr. Rankin had gone. The goods stayed in our attic for about 30 years. I cannot remember Mr. Rankin, but my brother, nearly five years older than myself, remembers him well.

When at our last Founders' Day, eleven years ago in 1932, Dr. Bechtel was appealing for pioneer pictures, I asked my brother to describe James Rankin. He said he was a man of studious habits, clean spoken, of an inventive turn of mind and of a type that would just fit in nicely as a church elder. He said that he had a son who was a timber surveyor and that the compass in our attic had been used in the northern woods by the son.

But we have not yet proved that the above James Rankin and James Rankin, the first elder of Calvary Church, were one and the same person.

I talked in 1932 with F. W. Osborne, 54 Seward avenue, whose recollections of Calvary Church go far back, and asked him what he knew about James Rankin, the first elder. He said he knew the old gentleman well, that he was a brass founder, lived on Eighteenth street, could remember distinctly one son with red hair, and a daughter, Grace, who was an artist.

I visited F. E. Rankin, attorney, 803 Hammond Building, Detroit. He said he knew James Rankin, the brass founder, and knew also of his son, John S. Rankin, the timber surveyor, and remembered that James had several children, among whom was Grace, an artist. He told me that John S. Rankin, the timber surveyor, died many years ago on an island in Georgian Bay. Mr. F. E. Rankin told me he was not related in any way and advised me to visit his older sister, Mrs. Timothy Edwards, of Washington, Mich., formerly Miss Anne Rankin. Mrs. Edwards was then 88 years of age, bright, intellectual, with memory as keen as ever. Mr. Edwards was 98 years of age (a retired Methodist minister) and possessing also a wonderful memory. Mrs. Edwards remembers well James Rankin, the brass founder who lived on Park street, and said that the mail of the two families used to get mixed. Just think, that's back in Civil War times. She remembers distinctly two of the daughters, Grace and Euphemia.

Rev. Timothy Edwards (98 years of age) told us he went up last year in an airplane, enjoyed it immensely and hoped to go again. Mrs. Downie asked Mrs. Edwards if she did not feel nervous about her husband going up in an airplane, and she replied: "No; I went up with him." Mrs. Edwards said that James Rankin moved from Park street to the western part of the city.

But we haven't yet conclusively proved our man.

Referring to the records of the Fort Street Presbyterian Church, we find James Rankin joined that church August 4th, 1850, and that he was dismissed to the First Presbyterian Church, Sept. 5th, 1857.

Making inquiry at the First Presbyterian Church the writer received the following reply:

First Presbyterian Church,
Woodward Avenue and Edmund Place,
Detroit, Michigan, May 19, 1932.
Mr. Wm. Downie,
4447 Vancouver Avenue, Detroit, Michigan.

Dear Mr. Downie.

We have been going into the records of the church, and discover that data so far back is not very complete nor satisfactory. Anyway, we will give you what we are able to find.

We find that Mr. and Mrs. James Rankin were dismissed from Fort Street Church to First Church September 5, 1857. They resided at 157 Park Avenue. Following are the names of their children: James, Jr., John S., Jeannette, Mary and Euphemia.

I cannot give you the record as to which church they were dismissed to or as to the death of any of them.

I hope that will serve your purpose.

Thanking you, I am

Very cordially yours,

CEM:FJL   C. E. MIERAS.

Since rendering me this splendid service eleven years ago Mr. C. E. Mieras of the First Presbyterian Church has been killed in an accident which we all deeply regret.

In the year 1875, Jas. Rankin disappears from the directory for good, but in 1874 his name appears, as does also Grace Rankin, artist, and also Robert C. Rankin, at 198 Eighteenth street. In 1875 they all disappear. In 1877, Robert C. reappears continually down to about 20 years ago, living at 81 Beecher street. Next door to this address I found Mr. Clark, who has lived in the neighborhood about 30 years. From him I learned that he knew Robert C. Rankin, and obtained the address of Jas. Rankin's grand-daughter, Mrs. Ennis Vernier Hyatt, 14600 Lauder avenue, Detroit. I visited Mrs. Hyatt. She gave me a photo of James Rankin and said that he had lived on Park street, Detroit, and had moved from Detroit to a 20-acre farm near Big Rapids, Mich., was superintendent of the Presbyterian Sunday School there, and remembered as a little girl taking him by the hand down the road to the Sunday School. She said he was of a very inventive nature. Mrs. Hyatt's two bothers, the grandsons of James Rankin, are John Vernier, 5547 Oregon avenue; Frank Vernier, 2527 Ferris avenue, and a sister, also James Rankin's grand-daughter, Dr. Jean A. Vernier, 41 East Willis Avenue, all of Detroit.

Mrs. Ennis Hyatt's mother's name was Euphemia. She remembers well her Aunt Grace, the artist, who died many years ago, and Robert C., whom she says was the red-haired boy described by Mr. Osborne.

Mr. James Rankin was the only James Rankin in the directory at the founding of the church, before it and for many years after.

Robert C. Rankin, the red-haired boy and the last living child, died about two years ago at Ecorse, Michigan.

I think I have left no doubt in your minds that the goods of James Rankin, the first elder, were stored in our attic 57 years ago.

Below is a replica of an advertisement taken from page 70 of city directory for the year 1861, the year the Civil War started:

J. & J. S. RANKIN
BRASS FOUNDERS
Brass Work of all Kinds
Brass Castings, Bell Hangings, etc.
Corner Congress and Third Sts.

DETROIT   MICHIGAN

Models Made to Order

MR. EBENEZER CHENEY, SECOND ELDER

Mr. Cheney lived at 233 Twentieth street. He had a wholesale and retail millinery store at 172 Woodward avenue. He died many years ago. He had a son, an electrical engineer, and three daughters. The writer's wife's brother, Robert Reid, of North Tonawanda, New York, worked for Mr. Cheney when he was a boy.

DAVID REID

David Reid was the father of the writer's wife and one of the early elders, his services dating back to the cottage near Michigan and Twenty-third streets. He died in November, 1874. The following remember David Reid as one of the first elders: Mrs. Agnes Telfer Boothroyd, 2106 Twentieth street, Detroit; Mrs. Wm. H. Blackford, 2762 Twenth-fourth street, Detroit, and Mrs. George P. Parsons, 9696 Lake Huron Drive, Port Huron, Mich. At the time of his death he was the teacher of the Adult Bible Class. Rev. Wm. Grandy performed the funeral ceremonies.

FIRST TRUSTEES

Samuel A. Plumer was a real estate man and builder of wide reputation and a man of splendid character, who contributed liberally with Mrs. Plumer to the church. John Plumer, a son, who died a few years ago, was well known in business circles as a fine business man with a splendid reputation. Mr. Plumer is survived by Mrs. Wm. H. Blackford, who, with Mr. Blackford, are wonderful contributors to Calvary Church. Mr. Blackford is an ex-trustee, very active as a trustee in this church when the first unit or auditorium was being built 25 years ago. Distance forbids Mr. and Mrs. Blackford attending regularly on account of their age. But they are wonderful contributors and come when they can. The Plumer room and piano are two of their numerous gifts. Mr. Blackford is president of the Detroit Casket Co., which he established 60 years ago and their home which they love was designed for Mrs. Blackford's grandfather over 100 years ago by one of Detroit's famous French architects. They both love Calvary Church. Their hearts are here.

John R. Gentle was an architect and builder and lived in Detroit many years, finally moving to California. He married a sister of the writer's wife. He has since died.

Bradford Smith was a school teacher. He died several years ago. He was a very fine gentleman and had a fine family. When the writer was about fifteen years of age Mr. Smith came into a store where the writer was working during vacation and engaged the latter in a friendly discussion of an algebra problem which the writer much enjoyed.

DAVID S. OSBORNE

David S. Osborne was a man of fine character and served Calvary Church well. He left a son, F. W. Osborne, of Buhl Sons & Co., Detroit, and a daughter, Mrs. George P. Parsons, 9696 Lake Huron Drive, Port Huron, Mich. Father and son have both departed this life.

DARWIN D. DAVIS

We know that he was a car accountant for the Michigan Central Railroad and in 1884 moved to Ypsilanti, Michigan, where he still held the same position with the railroad. He has since died.

ABEL SHOTWELL

Was a grocer on Nineteenth street. He died September 13th, 1888. The neighbors called him Honest Abe.

THE FIRST SUNDAY SCHOOL SUPERINTENDENT

Mr Walter P. Kellogg was the first superintendent. Every person speaks kindly of him. He and Mr. King owned a hardware store at 23 Monroe avenue in 1871. In 1878 he became branch manager here of the Rathbone, Sard Stove Co., of Buffalo, N. Y., which position he held until 1890, when he moved to Denver, Colorado. All trace of him from then was lost. The writer wrote to Mr. George Matheson, residing at Denver, in 1932, asking him to trace Mr. Kellogg in the directory after 1890. Mr. Matheson is the brother of Miss Elizabeth Matheson of our church, since deceased. Just before going to press the writer has received a photo of Mr. Kellogg. Mr. Matheson found that Mr. Kellogg had died Feb. 14th, 1918. He had been in the stove business under the name of Kellogg & Stokes Stove Co. in Denver. He traced a former partner, Harry Cope, who had a photograph, and said that he had often heard Mr. Kellogg speak of his former connections in Calvary Sunday School, Detroit. Mrs. Kellogg, his second wife, died shortly after Mr. Kellogg.

REV. WILLIAM GRANDY

Rev. William Grandy succeeded Dr. Atterbury and resigned in 1878 to take a pastorate at Tecumseh, Michigan. He was very much beloved in Calvary Church. There are still several people who remember him and speak very highly of him. He conducted the funeral services for Mrs. Downie's father, Elder David Reid. As a little girl she can remember him coming to their grief-striken home. At the present moment in 1932, as I am penning this paragraph, I am seated in the home of Mrs. Downie's sister in Toledo, Mrs. D. McPherson, whose husband has just been taken by death. Mrs. McPherson remembers well Rev. Grandy performing the funeral services for her father in 1874. Mr. McPherson and Mrs. McPherson were both past members and workers in the Butternut street church and were eagerly looking forward to being present Founders' Day at Calvary Church, June 12th, 1932. In trying to locate a picture of Dr. Grandy in 1932 the writer visited the church at Tecumseh where he preached 54 years before—found two people who knew him intimately and spoke very highly of him—Mrs. Slayton and Attorney Fred Cook, who both still attend the same church. They had no picture, but promised to make inquiries among the congregation for one. Rev. Grandy assisted in marrying Mrs. Slayton, who, by the way, years ago was the Sunday School teacher of Mrs. George Wright of our own Calvary Church.

At the time of going to press, not having yet heard from Mr. Cook or Mrs. Slayton, I presume neither of them has been successful.

The writer, knowing that Rev. Grandy took a pastorate at the Sioux City Presbyterian Church, Sioux City, Iowa, in 1884 (and not knowing the present pastor's name of that church or whether the church was still in existence), wrote to the postmaster of Sioux City enclosing a letter addressed to the pastor of the Sioux City church, requesting the same be delivered to him. In this letter the writer asked the pastor to make an appeal from the pulpit for a picture of Rev. Grandy, who had died Jan. 4th, 1885, at the age of 42 in Sioux City. The writer received the following two letters, showing his letter directed in care of the postmaster had done its work. The writer received from Miss Meta E. Grandy, accordingly, a photo of both her father and mother. Mrs. Grandy's picture will be shown on the screen Sunday, June 12th. (That of course was back in 1932.)

FIRST PRESBYTERIAN CHURCH
Sioux City, Iowa

Miss Meta Grandy,
2933 Jackson St.,
Sioux City, Iowa.

May 16, 1932.

Dear Miss Grandy:

I am sending the enclosed letter to you, and I am sure that if anybody can grant the request, you will be able to do so.

Faithfully yours,
P. E. BURTT.

Mr. Wm. Downie,
4447 Vancouver Ave.,
Detroit, Michigan.

2933 Jackson St.,
Sioux City, Iowa.
May 24, 1932.

Dear Mr. Downie:

Your letter of May 13, was sent across town to me in the letter I am enclosing from Dr. Burtt, our present minister.

It took some little time to get photographs that seemed to me would best suit your purpose.

We haven't any to spare, so I am insuring these and asking you to do the same when returning.

Father was pastor of this church only a short year, but he left an indelible mark.

Sincerely yours,
(Miss) META E. GRANDY.

P.S. Mother died in November, 1905.

The writer, knowing also that in the year 1873 Rev. Grandy had preached at Brighton, Mich., wrote to Rev. W. H. Simmons, the present pastor of the same church, requesting him to make an appeal from the pulpit for a photograph. This he did, with no success, and advised me to phone Miss Mable L. Lee, 167 Highland Avenue, Highland Park, Mich., which I did. Miss Lee advised me to write to Mr. Fred L. Dickey, of Kansas City, Kansas, and I received the following letter, which explains itself.

W. S. DICKEY CLAY MFG. CO.
Manufacturers of Clay Products
Kansas City, Mo.

Mr. William Downie, May 23, 1932.
4447 Vancouver Ave.,
Detroit, Michigan.
My dear Mr. Downie:

Your letter of the 22nd, addressed to my brother, the late Walter S. Dickey, has been referred to me for attention, and I am very happy to say that I can send you an excellent photograph of Rev. William Grandy, who was the pastor to whom you refer. He married my father's youngest sister, and four of their children are living. They are: William Frederick Grandy, Sioux City, Iowa, very well known in real estate and insurance business; Miss Meta E. Grandy, principal of the Bryant School, Sioux City; Mrs. G. P. Stratter, Sioux City, and Miss Adah G. Grandy, instructor in the State University of Minnesota at Minneapolis.

While I am confident any one of them would be glad to comply with your request, I can perhaps save a little time, as you seem to be in a hurry, by mailing the picture to you. It is at my home, but I will mail it to you tomorrow, and trust it will serve your purpose. I have another, so you need not return it. Mr. Grandy was a very devout man and greatly beloved for his beautiful Christian character.

Wishing you success in your undertaking, I am,
Cordially yours,
(MISS) M. LOUISE DICKEY.

The writer is happy to say that he received the photograph from Miss Dickey, and a cut made from the same appears in this history.

And so on Founder's Day at the 64th anniversary of Calvary Church we were pleased to receive and read to the congregation a letter from the children of Rev. Grandy of which the following is a copy.

2933 Jackson St.,
Sioux City, Iowa,
June 8, 1932.

Mr. William Downie,
4447 Vancouver Ave.,
Detroit, Michigan.

Dear Mr. Downie:

It is indeed a pleasure to send through you our good wishes to Calvary Presbyterian Church for Founder's Day, June 12, 1932.

May your church continue to grow in the future as it has in the past and may it continue to minister to its people and to be a power for good in the community.

We are proud of the fact that our father had a part in the upbuilding.
                W. F. Grandy,
                Mrs. G. P. Statler,
                Adah G. Grandy,
                Meta E. Grandy.

THE TORNADO OF JUNE 1875

On June 27th, 1875, on a Sunday afternoon a tornado struck Detroit around the then Calvary Church. Houses were blown down, trees were up-rooted, two horses were carried up into the air and killed. A babe was found dead in the streets. A boy was carried up into an elm tree and killed. Many persons lay wounded in the hospitals. That afternoon Rev. Grandy was out in the street, his clothing covered with blood, bandaging the bleeding wounded with bed quilts and assisting them into the ambulances. The writer can just remember that tornado and the two dead horses were carried past his parents' home the next morning on a truck on their way to Parker's tannery the last resting place of all Detroit horses.

In part 1 Robert McKinnell ably covered the pastorates of Dr. Barlow, Dr. Wolff and Dr. Shields.

In the year 1879, Rev. Grandy was succeeded by Rev. Geo. W. Barlow, D.D. Under his leadership the church flourished and to him and Mrs. Barlow is credited the erection of the new church at Michigan and Maybury Avenues. He continued as pastor till

1892. During his pastorate, on April 5th, 1886, Detroit had its greatest snow storm in all history. Snow was piled up six feet deep in front of the Newcomb Endicott & Company store on Woodward Avenue, now the north end of the J. L. Hudson Company store. After 10 o'clock in the morning no street car could run. All steam roads were stopped and the factories were all closed. But on account of the season, the snow disappeared about as fast as it came, and it was the greatest snow storm in Detroit that history records. The snow was 12 feet deep in some drifts. For official weather report see Detroit News and Detroit Free Press of April 6th, 1886, Burton Historical Library.

In 1893 Dr. Barlow was succeeded by Rev. Andrew T. Wolff, D.D., who resigned in 1894.

In 1895 Rev. W. Hamill Shields was installed and served till 1900 and is now the only living ex-pastor. Both Mr. and Mrs. Shields have in recent years paid us several visits, and we are always glad to welcome them not only as friends, but in honor of Rev. Shields' successful pastorate in Calvary Church.

CALVARY AT ITS VERY BEGINNING 1868

The first meetings were held in a little room over a grocery store on Harrison Avenue. Then the rear of a cottage was secured on Michigan Avenue near 23rd Street, where our present member Mrs. Wm. H. Blackford attended holding the hand of her big brother John Plumer, who later became a trustee and whose father and mother were charter members. This cottage was in reality the beginning as Harrison Avenue was not satisfactory, this authentic information coming to me from Mrs. Boothroyd who attended it. The front part of the cottage was a meat market and had a side entrance to the rear for the Sunday School. From information given us by Mrs. Blackford and Robert Reid (brother of the writer's wife) both attendants at this cottage Sunday School, we have here produced the artist's conception of this Sunday School cottage and we believe it to be a very close resemblance. Mrs. Agnes Boothroyd also a charter member who was deceased about three or four years ago verified this picture of the meat market mission as being quite correct.

From the above cottage Calvary moved in 1869 to the first church at the S.E. corner of Maybury Avenue and Butternut Street. It was demolished many years ago and is replaced by a dwelling.

WHO REMEMBERS THE BELL FALLING?

David Reid, of Rochester, Michigan, son of the early elder, tells us that one Sunday as the bell in the Butternut church was ringing, it broke away from its bearings, slid through the belfry, down the sloping room and crashed into the sidewalk on the Butternut side. No one was injured.

PERIOD FROM 1912 TO 1932

Referring back to Thursday evening, October 24th, 1912, the twelfth anniversary of Dr. Sutherland's pastorate, Mrs. Downie and the writer had the pleasure of being present at that event, although I was not a member then and Mrs. Downie had left several years before, when moving to another part of the city. At this celebration, considerable stress by many of the speakers was placed upon the changing conditions of the locality, the encroachment of packing houses and the influx of Slavic peoples and other foreigners with habits and customs out of tune with English speaking people, such as the members of Calvary Church.

THE PORTABLE CHAPEL ON VICKSBURG

OPENING OF GRAND RIVER AVENUE MISSION

From session minutes of Oct. 28, 1914, we find it was decided to open the mission located at the corner of Grand River and

Vicksburg Avenues on November 8th, services to start at 3 P.M., and to be held every Sunday. Dr. Jacques was asked to preach, and B. F. Matthews was appointed to secure dodgers advertising the event. Helen Downie played the piano for the Sunday school and continued for 15 years as pianist.

This mission was a portable wooden structure that had previously served as a Presbyterian mission away out Gratiot Avenue.

The services were soon changed from the afternoon to the morning, and David Scott preached, while Dr. Sutherland attended to the services in the Michigan Avenue church. The Sunday School was in charge of Dr. H. A. Currie, a very efficient superintendent. The chapel membership grew rapidly, so that it was decided to build an addition to it. Also it was agreed that the last services in Calvary Church on Michigan Avenue would be held on Nov. 12th, 1916, and preparations were being made for breaking ground for the new church. The services henceforth of all Calvary members were to be held in the chapel until the new church would be completed.

Ground was broken for the new church Oct. 8th, 1916. Mr. Warren E. Brinkerhoff, on behalf of the building committee, introduced Mr. John Mead (father of Mrs. Dr. H. A. Currie) as the one selected to turn the first sod. Those taking part in the ceremony were: Dr. Sutherland, David C. Scott, Dr. Dickie, Dr. Gantz, Dr. J. M. Barclay, Dr. Edward Pence, Dr. Wm. Jacques and Dr. Wm. S. Buck. Special music was rendered by the choir, under the direction of C. Y. Smith.

The cornerstone was laid Sept. 23rd, 1917. Services started at 3 p.m., with Dr. D. I. Sutherland presiding. The programme was as follows: Opening prayer, Rev. Jas. H. McDonald; scripture lesson by Rev. T. G. Sykes; addresses by Dr. Joseph Vance, Rev. Minot C. Morgan, Rev. W. H. Jameson, Rev. J. M. Barclay, D.D., and David C. Scott. Prayer was offered by Dr. Clinton W. Lowrie. The cornerstone was laid by the pastor, Dr. D. I. Sutherland, assisted by Elders John Munroe and Walter E. Adams. A special prayer of consecration was offered by Dr. J. M. Barclay, who was also present at the laying of the cornerstone of the old church on Michigan Avenue in 1887. A tribute was tendered to Mrs. Barlow, widow of former Pastor Dr. George W. Barlow, and Mrs. Sutherland, the entire congregation rising to their feet and giving the Chautauqua salute with their handkerchiefs. The following articles were ordered placed in the box: the Holy Bible, Presbyterian Hymnal, historical sketch of Calvary Church by the pastor, Dr. Sutherland, and also a sketch that had been placed in the cornerstone of the old building on Michigan Avenue by the Rev. George W. Barlow, deceased; also a copy of the old Calvary Chimes, a copy of the Auburn Seminary records, a copy of the Continent and also a copy of two of our daily papers, the Detroit Free Press and the Detroit Journal. The writer personally had this strong box made and sealed with metal that will never rust and will last for all time, as far as the elements are concerned. The box on Michigan Avenue was made of tin and of course was all rusted and punctured. This box on Grand River Avenue should stand all weathers for all time being made of nonrust metal.

The dedication of the new church was on Sunday, November 17th, 1918, at 3 p.m. The services consisted of music under the direction of Minor A. Gregg, a very efficient organist, and the following:

Scripture reading—Rev. J. D. MacDonald, D.D.

Words of dedication—Led by Rev. R. M. Huston, D.D

Prayer of dedication—Rev. Hugh Jack, D.D.

Prayer of consecration—Rev. Angus H. Cameron, D.D.

Sermon—Rev. Joseph A. Vance, D.D.

Benediction.

THE GRAND RIVER BUILDING IN 1931

The following were the officers of the church at that time:

Session—B. F. Mathews, clerk; W. E. Adams, treasurer; T. T. Pomeroy, Chas. Pennington, John Munro, John Mead, Edward S. Clark, A. A. Sutherland.

Trustees—Harry J. Mackie, president; John Sandick, vice-president; Wm. Downie, treasurer; Chas. Lakin, financial secretary; Mark B. Coonley, secretary; Adam McKendrick, Dr. H. A. Currie, Vaughan Reid and Dave Matthews.

Building committee—Adam McKendrick, chairman; John Sandick, Charles Lakin, William Downie; superintendent of construction, Warren E. Brinkerhoff.

The cost of the church and pews was approximately $60,000 and the lots $10,000, or a total of $70,000. On the day of dedication there was a mortgage of $22,000 on the church. On that day $30,000 in pledges was raised, and the entire debt of the church was quickly wiped out. On the Wednesday preceding the dedication we gave a pre-dedication supper for 25c, the largest meal ever served in Calvary Church. We actually fed (according to the count of tickets taken in) between 1,500 and 1,600 people. Six hundred pounds of roast beef and 10 bushels of potatoes were quickly consumed and more food brought in and we made a nice profit. Dr. McGarrah of Philadelphia wanted us to give a good supper at a very low price to get the multitude in and interest them in the new church. Much food was donated by liberal merchants in the community. While a few hundred of our guests did not and could not enjoy the advertised menu, still the writer can vouch that everybody got a big 25c worth and several hundred more guests came than we had any way of anticipating, not having sold tickets in advance.

REINCORPORATION

It was discovered in the year 1916 that the 30-year charter of the church had expired and immediately steps were taken to reincorporate the church, so that the business of the latter could be transacted legally. This matter was hastened, as the congregation had received an offer to buy the church property on Michigan Avenue. Consequently, in 1916 the church was reincorporated and new by-laws passed. (See pages 180-188, Congregational Records, 1916.)

SALE OF THE CHURCH

Next door east of the church property stood the buildings of Swift & Co., meat packers, and immediately east of them was the property of Parker-Webb & Co., meat packers. The latter needed more room, and in order to acquire the Swift property they proposed to buy the Calvary Church property, move Swift & Co. on to it, and they (Parker, Webb & Co.) to occupy the Swift property. Consequently, in 1916 Parker, Webb & Co. offered the church $25,100 for the church property. This offer was accepted by the trustees, subject to the approval of the congregation, which was given at a congregational meeting held March 16th, 1916. (See Congregation Record, page 188, 1916). A motion was made and carried to appoint a committee to request the Presbytery to establish a mission in this district to care for those who could not attend services at the proposed new location at Grand River and Vicksburg Avenues.

THE FIRE

When Parker, Webb & Co. purchased the property, the arrangement was that we should hold services in the church until the new building was completed. But in the fall of 1916 Parker, Webb & Co. were anxious to have possession of the church property immediately. They offered to store the organ, pews and all belongings of the church in the second story of their garage and pay $250 to the church if the latter would vacate the premises and give them possession at once. Consequently, all belongings of the church were placed in the Parker, Webb & Co. building, there to be kept until the new church would be finished and the church discontinued services Nov. 12, 1916, on Michigan Avenue, with future services to be held in the enlarged chapel until the completion of the new church. This move reduced the expenses, which were now causing the church to go behind financially in the rapidly changing environment.

But one night the building caught fire and every belonging including nearly every record of Calvary Church was destroyed (except the organ, which had been placed in another part of the building not reached by the fire) and the Mead marble baptismal font. The latter, however, was badly scorched by smoke. An Italian sculptor chiseled off the surface of the font to a depth that the smoke had penetrated, completely restoring its beauty. While the church collected $3,850 insurance, this amount did not cover the loss in full, on account of the pews being burned, it being remembered that the Great War had started and the price of lumber was mounting.

THE FAMOUS CHOIR IN THE MICHIGAN AVE. CHURCH

BUILDING THE NEW CHURCH

The writer has stated before that the church was sold for $25,100. Out of this a commission of $753 was paid, and the rapidly changing condition of the locality on account of the encroachment of obnoxious packing house business and foreign population had caused the church to go behind financially to the amount of $1,000, so that out of the sale of the church there was left about $23,347.

GETTING THE LOAN DURING THE FIRST WORLD WAR

Uncle Sam had issued orders to the banks that no money was to be loaned for building purposes, except in cases of absolute necessity. The trustees bargained for many weeks with banks and individuals with no success, and we could not for months find an excavator who had faith enough in our credit to dig our basement. It looked very discouraging. Finally in a short space of time $5,000 in dividends on account of war profits came from the National Twist Drill Co. stock donated by George Mead. The trustees appointed Adam McKendrick, W. E. Brinkeroff and the writer to interview the church extension committee, and we secured a gift of $2,000, which was given to us out of the sale of the old Second Avenue Presbyterian Church which is now called the Central Presbyterian Church located at Grand River and Second Avenues. Mr. Sandick, Mr. McKendrick and the writer were appointed to adjust the fire loss with the appraisers, and we secured $3,850. By some good bargaining the trustees sold some National Twist Drill stock at $60.25 per share (a top notch price), realizing $13,857, and with the accumulation of the above sums we needed just about $22,000 more to complete the building and pews and pay for the lots. By this time the Peninsular State Bank officers began to have faith in us and the necessity of our proposition, and granted us the loan. And Calvary Church kept her word. She never defaulted and she never contracted obligations until she could clearly see her way to pay back in full on time.

The financial committee appointed to finance the church building consisted of: the writer, chairman; Adam McKendrick, Dave H. Matthews, John Sandick and H. J. Mackie. The splendid cooperation and determined effort of every man on the board meant a lot to the above committee.

But why was the church built just as it was built? Well, in the first place, we were mighty short of money. We didn't know that we were going to have the good luck of fat Twist Drill dividends, nor did we dream when we started drawing plans that we would ever sell the stock at such an excessive price, nor that we would receive a gift of $2,000 from the Church Extension Committee. Therefore, economy was the watchword. It was apparent to Adam McKendrick, the master mind on practical building matters, that to secure the maximum value for every dollar spent, practically a replica of the old church was necessary, with the exception of some wider aisles, etc., in order to use the original pews, which if discarded, would have meant a loss of about $4,500. Also a gymnasium was wanted and to save a large sum on masonry the footings of the walls of the church were made to rest a considerable distance above the floor level of the gymnasium, thus being just as secure as though they had gone down all the way, as the earth under the galleries in the gym was not excavated, but allowed to remain, thus effecting another economy.

Mr. Sandick became a member of the building committee a short time after the other three members and rendered valuable assistance.

Charles Lakin, electrical engineer, also aided greatly with advice and services.

Warren E. Brinkerhoff, a civil engineer of long standing, executed stress diagrams of all trusses and rechecked all cross sections of materials for his own satisfaction, although this work had all previously been done by an able firm of engineers, but Mr. Brinkerhoff wished to be doubly sure. Don't ever be afraid of Calvary Church falling down.

Mr. Brinkerhoff's mathematical training was that of a structural engineer. He was the engineer of the Detroit Bridge and Iron works. He analyzed every section of steel that went into a bridge or roof truss, determined how many tons stress (tension or compression) that piece withstood and designed an appropriate cross section to withstand that particular strain. John Sandick was a thoroughly practical builder. Charles Lakin was an electrical engineer of ability. Adam McKendrick was a builder of large experience and practical, economical ideas who was exceptionally valuable in the construction of the church. The writer's training has been largely identical with that of Mr. Brinkerhoff so it will be readily seen that the steel trusses in the attic are not guess work. A melancholy fact remains—out of the five only Adam McKendrick and the writer remain. However, fortunately, the church is well endowed with a retinue of younger, well seasoned men who are perfectly capable of carrying on the torch but always remember that all experience and advice with which we older fellows may help you in a tight spot are always gladly at your command.

Before leaving this subject, let me recall to you that on account of the World War No. 1 labor and materials were at the highest price in history.

SPIRITUAL GROWTH OF THE CHURCH

With the removal of the church to the enlarged chapel in November, 1916, Calvary Curch began to grow and prosper greatly, both in membership and financially. She gave generously to missions. She gave liberally to the poor. Upon moving from the chapel next door to the finished church, her prosperity continued in leaps and bounds. All of this was under the able leadership of our deceased beloved pastor, Dr. D. I. Sutherland, a man of wonderful personality, natty, big hearted, a true Christian gentleman, a man of great wit and humor, an extemporaneous speaker of renown, a man who loved fun, who was serious when the occasion demanded, a man of the common people, but an aristocrat. His faults (if he had any) were virtues, for they made people laugh. He was the young people's idol. It was commonly understood that he united more couples in marriage than any other minister.

The Young People's Society of Christian Endeavor prospered greatly in the church.

The Calvary Guards (originally organized by Mr. Selover and Wm. Seldon, Junior) were revived and gave Calvary Church wonderful advertising as a first class basketball team, traveling all over the state winning trophies and creating much favorable newspaper comment. Elders Charles Pennington, A. E. Duncan and Ex-Trustee Daniel A. McDonald were the teachers of the Calvary Guards Class.

The Kolah Club of young ladies, while a social organizaton, has unostentatiously done splendid work with the poor and distressed. Kolah is an Indian word meaning friendly.

The Sunday School grew and prospered under the able leadership of Dr. H. A. Currie, the first superintendent in the little chapel, who sowed the seeds for its wonderful future under the splendid officers who succeeded him.

The Ladies' Aid and Missionary Societies later combined into one society, known as the Women's Union, have done wonderful work, both along missionary lines and in assisting the trustees with the the financial burdens of the church.

One of the early enterprises of the church after its completion was giving returns at the presidential election in 1920. The Western Union Co. ran a wire into the gymnasium. A fine programme, alternating with the election returns, lasted until midnight. Nathan Rumney, traffic manager of the Detroit United Railway and an ex-trustee, placed large posters on the front fender of about every other Grand River car election day. The result was the gymnasium was packed with people from all parts of the city.

GIFTS

The beautiful carved pulpit furniture was the gift of Mrs. Margaret Tireman just as the new church was completed. All of the memorial windows tell their own story with each inscription.

Space forbids me to attempt enumerating all of the multitudinous individuals that have given liberally to Calvary Church of their time and money or to make honorable mention individually of her splendid past and present list of officers, both among the men and women, or among the young people. But it is refreshing to know that there are still several individuals attending Calvary Church or contributing to her support in the year 1932 who were attending the old church on Michigan Avenue. I cannot recall all of these persons, but off hand those who come to my mind are Dr. and Mrs. H. A. Currie (Mrs. Currie's father was Mr. John Mead, an old officer and worker), Mr. and Mrs. Wm. Blackford (Mrs. Blackford's father was Samuel Plumer), a former trustee; Mrs. Annie Johnson, herself Sunday School treasurer in the old church (father was Wm. H. Seldon, Sr., and her brother, William Seldon, Jr., both splendid supporters of the church in every way), Mr. and Mrs. Ben Matthews, Mr. and Mrs. Dave Matthews, Mr. H. J. Mackie, ex-trustee, and Grace Mackie, Mr. Adams, Mrs. Wescott, Mr. and Mrs. Peter Grant, Mary Gibson, Mrs. E. B. Gregor, Mr. and Mrs. Ed. Knight, Mrs. Wm. L. Newkirk, Mrs. Richardson, whose father was Robert Lytle, trustee; Miss Lottie Crosby, Mr. A. A. Sutherland, Mr. and Mrs. Clarence Metcalfe, Mr. and Mrs. Vaughn Reid, Mrs. Margaret Coulton and T. Burrows, Mark B. Coonley, ex-trustee, and his mother, Mrs. Helen Coonley, Mr. and Mrs. Stoddard, the McKenzies, the Hustons, Mrs. Alex. Nelson, Mrs. Anna Purdon and May Lux. Another familiar name is that of Mr. and Mrs. John McKerchey, who have given liberally to Calvary. We are always glad to have them drop in and see us. But alas many since of the above list have gone to their long reward.

Undoubtedly I have omitted some, as it is impossible to remember all, so please pardon me. It is not intentional.

KINDERGARTEN

Shortly after the opening of the chapel, Mrs. Barlow conducted the kindergarten department of the Sunday School, thus renewing her work of many years before.

OTHER DENOMINATIONS

From the foregoing it will be seen that Calvary had a prosperous, mounting future for many years after moving to the new location. The territory was new and growing rapidly. But in the course of time other denominations sprang up in this district, some of which were the Lutheran Church across the road, the Episcopal Church at the Boulevard, the Congregational Church at Warren and the Boulevard, the Northwestern Baptist Church on Grand River Avenue, the Nardin Park Methodist Church, the Fourteenth Avenue Baptist Church and the Pilgrim Congregational Church on Linwood Avenue.

These different churches drew back home many of their own people, who otherwise would have continued in Calvary. And so there was bound to be some recession from the peak previously reached. However, the great work of Calvary Church continued, with Dr. Sutherland as pastor, ably assisted by Mrs. Sutherland, who took a very active part in the work.

OUR MISFORTUNE

My Dad used to say to us boys—"Don't pay your bills when they are due. Go one better, pay before they are due and your credit will rocket sky high." Back in the early life of the Grand River Church here at Vicksburg Ave., a little over twenty years ago, we had a flood in the spring of the year from excessive rains. Basements were flooded everywhere. Of course the church sewerage ran east and connected with the lateral sewer in the alley which was connected with the sewer in the alley between Vicksburg and Virginia Park Avenues. This was laid out according to city orders but the alley sewers were far too small, the city engineers not having anticipated the rapid growth of houses eastwardly on both Vicksburg and Virginia Park Avenues. Consequently one day the basement of the church (that is the gymnasium) was flooded. Pianos, tables, chairs, etc., were floating in all directions. The oak floor was ruined. It was a sorrowful, disheartening mess. But a squad of determined faithful members gritted their teeth, rolled up their sleeves and cleaned it all up and it was some job. A large expense confronted us. A complete new oak floor had to be laid, new painting done, the entire internal sewerage of crocks and pipes of the building reversed so as to run toward the Grand River end of the building instead of the alley end.

The writer and Mr. Walker immediately contacted the cashier of the Peninsular Bank from whom we had received our loan of $22,000.00 and which we were paying on away ahead of time and had reduced to about four or five thousand dollars. We explained to him our dilemma and told him we needed money at once. He looked up our loan. "Why" he said, "Your credit is A-1. You are paid up away ahead of time. Loan granted without even being referred to the Board."

At once we contacted at the City Hall Mr. Martin, commissioner of Public Works and explained to him the situation. Without any argument or waste of words he said "I will have a gang out at Calvary Church tomorrow morning and connect your sewerage with the main sewer on the south side of Grand River Avenue." And he kept his word. They tunneled from the north side of Grand River under the street car tracks to the sewer on the south side and then connected all of our sewerage to it so from that day on there has been no danger of flood. This work took several weeks and cost the city of Detroit several hundred dollars for which there was no charge to Calvary Church.

THEIR TRAGEDY

In the early part of Dr. and Mrs. Sutherland's labors in the new church, a great sorrow overtook them. Their son, John, was called home. This was a great shock, but bravely they both bore up. After a while Mrs. Sutherland's health became impaired, so that she had to relinquish the greater part of her activity in the church. But on and on D. I. Sutherland fought the battles of life. Good, fearless soldier that he was, nothing daunted him.

Full of ambition, unbounded energy, on the go day and night, scarcely ever stopping, with health beginning to decline, suddenly he received the blow that was the beginning of the end. Angus, his son, had passed away; Angus, the physician of great promise, upon whom he doted. He never survived the shock.

Every day of his life he tried to make himself believe that he was conquering, but slowly and surely the end was coming. While to the public he was brave and smiled, yet he was dying of a broken heart. Under these circumstances his health impaired, and under gigantic mental anguish he carried on with tremendous energy, trying to comfort the sorrowing when his own heart was breaking. On the 28th of June 1930 (Saturday), he spent the day at the writer's Summer cottage with Mrs. Sutherland and daughter Olive. On the way home he was stricken. Just before leaving, he said that "the next day he would preach and leave on his vacation Monday, and he wished to preach to his congregation his best sermon, that would leave a kindly remembrance of him while he was away." The sermon was not preached. He died Monday, June 30th, 1930. But who could have other than a kind remembrance of Dr. Sutherland? His body lay in state in Calvary Church from 11 a.m. until the funeral service. All this time there was a steady flow of his friends, who came for the last glimpse of this remarkable man. The rich, the poor, and people of all nationalities and denominations poured into the church to do the last honors. He was buried on the second day of July 1930 in Grand Lawn Cemetery.

The following was taken from the Detroit Free Press, Tuesday, July 1st, 1930:

"Funeral services for Rev. David Innes Sutherland, D.D., for 30 years pastor of the Calvary Presbyterian Church, will be held at the church at 2 p.m., Wednesday. The body will lie in state from 11 a.m. until the services, and burial will be in Grand Lawn Cemetery. Dr. Sutherland died early Monday morning of a heart attack.

"He was born in Hamilton, Ont., May 17, 1861, coming to take the pastorate of Calvary Church in October, 1900. In the late 1880's he married Jean Wells Monroe of Ingersoll, Ont. Three children were born: Olive, now principal in Northern High School;

John, who died in 1917, and Dr. Angus P. Sutherland who died two years ago.

"Surviving are the widow, also the daughter, Miss Olive Sutherland, and three grandchildren, Jane, David and John, all of Detroit.

"Dr. Sutherland was very prominent in Masonry. He was a thirty-third degree Mason and member of Union Lodge No. 3, F. and A. M.; Damascus Commandery No. 42, Knights Templar; Detroit Consistory, Scottish Rite Masons, and honorary member of the Supreme Council of the Northern Jurisdiction of Masons. He was also a member of the Royal Order of Scotland and of Moslem Temple, Nobles of the Mystic Shrine.

"Arrangements for the funeral services at the church will be under supervision of Dr. T. G. Sykes, and the services will be held under auspices of Union Lodge. The body will be escorted to the cemetery by a uniformed detachment of Damascus Commandery."

Extracts from the Detroit News, Monday, June 30, 1930.

"He was 69 years old. The family moved to Ingersoll when he was a boy, and his education was begun at the Collegiate Institute at that place. Later he attended a private school at Auburn, N. Y., and then the Auburn Theological School, from which he was graduated in 1895. He received the degree of D.D. from Alma College in 1924."

And so a great man had gone.

The huge work of disposing of the Michigan Ave. church and building the main auditorium and gymnasium on Grand River Ave. together with the shifting of the congregation to the new location was accomplished under the masterful leadership of Dr. Sutherland during his thirty years pastorate but the heart of Calvary was crushed; a pall came over the congregation. It seemed like Calvary no more. But the spirit of Dr. Sutherland was marching on, beckoning to his congregation and saying: "On with my work."

In the course of a few months, Rev. Leslie A. Bechtel, D.D., of Superior, Wisconsin, was called by the unanimous vote of the congregation to succeed Dr. Sutherland. The choice of Dr. Bechtel was recommended by the commitee appointed to select applicants for the position. The committee consisted of L. J. Armstrong,

Albert E. Duncan, John Sandick, Vincent Palmer, Dr. H. A. Currie, Mrs. Frederick Woolfenden and Mrs. Nina Purington.

DR. BECHTEL

The following is a synopsis of Dr. Bechtel's life prior to his coming to Calvary Presbyterian Church:

Leslie A. Bechtel—Born, Victoria, B. C.; early life spent in Butte, Montana. Colleges—Montana State College, 1904-07; University of Wisconsin, 1907-10, A.B. Seminary—Union Theological, New York, N.Y., 1910-13, B.D. Postgraduate work—Columbia University, Cambridge University, University of Wisconsin. D.D. from Carroll College, 1923.

Pastorates—Immanuel Presbyterian Church, Butte, Montana, 1913-1916; student pastor, University of Wisconsin, Madison, 1916-1917; First Presbyterian Church, Reedsburg, Wis., 1917-1919; Hammond Avenue Presbyterian Church, Superior, Wisconsin, 1919-1931.

Married—1913, to Gertrude Egert of Lyndhurst, N. J. Children: Gertrude Marguerite, Lyla Elvira, Leslie Andrew, Jr., William Russell.

The members of the congregation were greatly pleased with Dr. Bechtel's trial sermon, and his personality appealed to them, with the result that he was called to the pastorate formerly held by Dr. Sutherland, as above stated.

Dr. Bechtel was installed April 23rd, 1931 with Alfred S. Nickless, D.D., moderator, presiding. The services consisted of an organ prelude by Ruth Alina Sloan; prayer by Dr. H. M. Noble, Howell, Mich.; anthem by Mark Andrews; scripture reading by Rev. Geo. D. Jeffrey; sermon, Rev. Ralph C. McAfee; charge to the congregation by Rev. Wm. T. Jacques; charge to the pastor by Rev. Frank Fitt, and Benediction.

A reception was tendered to Dr. and Mrs. Bechtel immediately following installation services.

Dr. Bechtel's educational background and natural abilty made him eminently qualified for the position; but one thing that counts for more than that is his tender, reverential attitude toward the memory of our beloved, deceased pastor. And Dr. Bechtel has shown a wonderfully generous disposition in wishing to stay in the shadow, that Dr. Sutherland's memory should eclipse all. And so Dr. Bechtel has endeared himself to this congregation, and the work of Dr. Sutherland is going on and on under the splendid leadership of Dr. Bechtel. Isn't this just what Dr. Sutherland would wish? And how could we please Dr. Sutherland more than by giving Dr. Bechtel a helping hand? If we criticize, let it always be honest, constructive criticism, given in the Christian spirit for the sole purpose of building up, and never with the idea of hindering or tearing down.

The present officers of the church 1932 are as follows:

SESSION

*A. A. Sutherland, W. G. Winchester, *H. R. McKenzie.
*Life members of the Session.

A. W. Church, S. A. Dodge, John Tillman, Joseph H. Jenkin, E. H. Knight, David Matthews, George Wright, A. E. Duncan, Lawrence W. Downie; B. F. Matthews, clerk; G. H. Rickels, J. J. Sandick, David Hall, Robert May, P. F. Reuss.

DEACONS

Vincent C. Palmer, president; Mrs. Helen Rice, William Downie, Jr., Thomas Burrows, Mrs. N. A. Carson, Robert Tennant.

TRUSTEES

George H. Willett, president; Dr. J. W. Hoffman, treasurer; G. W. Beasley, financial secretary; J. M. Hollinger, L. J. Armstrong, A. R. Morison, Adam McKendrick, M. A. Schilling, Fred Woolfenden.

SECRETARY TO THE MINISTER

Miss Carolyn Hoffman.

The next big move is to complete the D. I. Sutherland memorial on the vacant lot next to the church. This was the ultimate aim of the trustees when the present church was built. Opinions have differed in the past regarding the building of this addition under too heavy a mortgage. But the present plan to build the first story on a pay-as-you-go, or cash plan, is sound.

When the next historian writes the following period of Calvary Church, I hope that he gets as big a thrill as I have gotten. I am sure he will have big things to write about, but I hope his time for preparing his copy will not be so limited as mine has been. (This concludes the history written by the writer in 1932.)

WILLIAM DOWNIE

Again as stated in the foreword it so happens that the author of the history written in 1932 has been assigned the task of finishing the history of Calvary Church through its seventy-five years of of existence, which deals in the remaining pages with the pastorate of Dr. Bechtel and a most glorious chapter of accomplishments it will turn out to be.

Dr. Bechtel had been installed only about one year when he arranged for the 63rd celebration of Founders' Day largely to honor the memory of Dr. Sutherland. The programme was as follows: Miner Gregg was the guest organist. Invocation, Rev. Thos. G. Sykes. Prayer, Rev. L. L. Evans. Quartette, B. F. Matthews, Harry Harrison, Mrs. Elizabeth Partrige and Mrs. Elizabeth Cardinal. Address, Rev. Edward H. Pence. Address, Rev. Hugh Jack. Illustrated address, Robt. McKinnell. Address, Rev. Thos. G. Sykes.

Mr. J. T. Wing, old time friend of Dr. Sutherland, presented a plaque installed on the wall of the auditorium to the memory of Dr. Sutherland. The memorial was unveiled by the three grandchildren of Dr. Sutherland and the donor of the plaque was introduced by the writer.

One of the chief things to be accomplished was the building of the Sutherland Memorial on the lot adjoining the main auditorium. Several propositions had been examined previously and finally rejected as impractical. The financial crash of 1929 was sinking deeper and deeper. Soon was to follow the closing of the banks causing financial devastation to all of our congregation and absolute financial ruin to many. No one escaped. On account of deflation building now would be cheaper than to wait but money not so easy to get. Calvary has always been a progressive church but also a conservative one. Her policy before tackling a problem has been not to become involved unless all the way down the track were clear. Enthusiasm is grand but without a safety valve is also dangerous. So the best judgment in Calvary Church was to build the basement and first floor, omit the third floor (as previously planned) entirely and sell bonds to our own congregation, in other words a pay as you go plan. In this way it would neither be too large a proposition that would harass our congregation or place the church property in jeopardy through mortgage foreclosure. The bonds were quickly sold and redeemed on time and thus was added about $20,354.32 to the value of Calvary real estate which included an entire new furnace that was badly needed. A temporary roof was built over the new portion until a later day when the whole Sutherland Memorial could be finished.

The following was the order of services for Sunday, June 12th, 1932, when ground was broken for the new Sutherland Memorial.

SECOND ANNUAL FOUNDERS DAY
1868-1932
SUNDAY, JUNE 12, 1932
MORNING WORSHIP, 10:30

Organ Prelude—"St. Cecelia" .... *Gounod*
Processional Hymn .... No. 117
Doxology
Invocation and Lord's Prayer
Scripture .... Psalm 90
Reception of Members
Anthem
Prayer
Offertory
Communion Hymn .... No. 292
The Communion
Sermon—Dr. A. F. McGarrah, Philadelphia, Pa.
Hymn .... No. 391
Benediction
Benediction Response

EVENING WORSHIP, 7:30

Organ Prelude—"Pastorale" .... *Bach*
Processional Hymn .... No. 157
Doxology
Invocation and Lord's Prayer
Scripture .... John 14
Anthem
Prayer

Hymn ....No. 422
Offertory
"The Old Family Album"..........Explanations by Ben. F. Matthews
Hymn ....No. 724
Sermon—Dr. A. F. McGarrah, Philadelphia, Pa.
Hymn—"Blest Be the Tie that Binds"..No. 345
Benediction
Benediction Response

    The cut following shows the ceremony of breaking the ground for the Sutherland Memorial. Mr. Benjamin F. Matthews with spade in hand is softening the soil so that Mrs. D. I. Sutherland

BREAKING GROUND FOR SUTHERLAND MEMORIAL
JUNE, 1932

(to the right and seated) may turn over the sod. In this she was assisted by the three children of Dr. and Mrs. Angus P. Sutherland, Jean, David and John. Dr. Angus P. Sutherland was the late lamented son of Dr. and Mrs. D. I. Sutherland. To the extreme right is Mr. Geo. H. Willett, chairman of the Board of Trustees. This was an extremely happy moment for Mrs. D. I. Sutherland as it was also for Dr. Bechtel, whose energy and strict adherence to safe financing has made the project possible.

Laying of Corner Stone Sunday, Oct. 16th, 1932

No. 1. Dr. Bechtel
No. 2. L. J. Armstrong
No. 3. Miss Olive Sutherland
No. 4. Jean Sutherland
No. 5. David Sutherland
No. 6. John Sutherland
No. 7. B. F. Matthews

TRIBUTE TO MRS. SUTHERLAND
CALVARY PRESBYTERIAN CHURCH
DETROIT, MICHIGAN

At a meeting of the Session held on September 7, 1932, upon a motion made and duly supported, the Clerk of Session was authorized to procure suitable data upon the life and activities of Mrs. Jean Munro Sutherland, wife of the late Rev. D. I. Sutherland, D.D., and a resolution portraying the splendid work and the untiring efforts of Mrs. Sutherland in the different departments of the church.

Mrs. Sutherland was the youngest child of John Munro and his wife, Ann Price Munro, long since deceased. She was born in Ingersoll, Ontario, on the 21st of June, 1862, and was married to David Innis Sutherland on September 24, 1885.

When their family was very small, Mr. Sutherland entered the Theological Seminary at Auburn, New York, to study for the Christian ministry. 'Twas then that Mrs. Sutherland showed her worth as a young Christian mother in making everything as pleasant and comfortable for him as their limited financial condition would permit. About this time John, the youngest of the family, was born. Yet those very strenuous times were acknowledged by her to be among the happiest years of her life. She used to make it more pleasant for the other students and their young wives who used to gather around the home of the Sutherlands on Sunday afternoons and sing hymns while she played the organ. She also used to have her children gather in the nursery promptly at 9 o'clock every morning to receive their early educational training at her hand. She also took an active interest in the studies of her husband. As a minister's wife, she was indefatigable in all the church activities in their separate organizations.

For five years in the First Presbyterian Church at Susquehanna, Pennsylvania, and for twenty-five years at Calvary Church, Detroit, Michigan, the Women's Missionary Societies and Study Clubs received a generous portion of her time.

In the Christian Endeavor Societies, both senior and junior, she was always their counsellor and advisor. She was one of the chief promoters in the Women's Union of Calvary Church. She also was a teacher in Sunday School and was actively interested in the girls' clubs.

She had been honored with a life membership in the Presbyterian Society, and one time president of the Kenjockety. With all the duties of the aforesaid organizations which data can be vouched for undoubtedly in the minutes of the different organizations of the church, which the writer had not access to. She never neglected her duties as a faithful helpmate to her devoted companion or her beloved children, two of whom have passed on—Dr. Angus and John Sutherland.

Mrs. Sutherland passed to her reward on July 18, 1932, and was buried with her husband and two sons at Grandlawn Cemetery.

* * *

Therefore be it resolved that we, the members of the Session, and Rev. L. A. Bechtel as Moderator, do cause to be placed upon the records of the Session book the above data in commemoration of this once active life in our church activities. And be it further resolved that as the Almighty God has seen fit to remove this his servant from our midst that we, the minister and elders of our church, feel that we bespeak the sentiment of the congregation and more particularly the ladies with whom she came in personal contact, when we commend her virtues as a living example for us all to follow.

We also commend to His loving care all those who mourn her passing, more particularly the daughters and grandchildren, and may His watchful eye ever guide them in the future as in the past. May God grant those children to grow up to perpetuate the name and memory of their illustrious forbears.

SESSION OF CALVARY CHURCH,
B. F. Matthews,
Clerk of Session.

SUNDAY SCHOOL SUPERINTENDENTS FROM 1868-1943

W. P. Kellogg	Wm. S. Mitchell
H. Kirke White	Harry Mackie
Chas. G. Brownell	Chas. Pennington
John Austin	Dr. Harry A. Currie
Jas. G. Giauque	J. Blackall
W. A. Torney	W. R. Vender
Robt. Kerr	W. T. Leitheiser
Edward David	Dr. C. A. Paull
C. T. Duffie	Rev. Llewelyn Evans
John Munroe	G. W. Beasley
Bradford Smith	L. J. Armstrong
Arthur A. Higginson	Lawrence W. Downie
Robt. McKinnell	John Barry
Harry W. Harrison	Rev. James W. MacElree

THE LEADERSHIP OF CALVARY YEAR 1943
THE SESSSION

Dr. John W. Hoffman, Vice-Moderator

CLASS OF 1943	CLASS of 1944	CLASS OF 1945
A. B. McColl	S. A. Dodge, Clerk	John Fraser
H. W. Sherwood	Vincent C. Palmer	Paul Spielvogel
John Blair	John A. Jones	Russell Armstrong
William Moyer	J. M. Hollinger	Robert Church
A. E. Duncan	Lester Downie	Charles E. Bishop
James Y. Harper	Henry Bechtel	William Williamson
Charles Stickles	George Wilson	G. W. Beasley
Harold Welsh	Howard Galbraith	Elwood Manns

THE TRUSTEES

CLASS OF 1943	CLASS OF 1944	CLASS OF 1945
A. B. McColl, Treas.	L. J. Armstrong	S. A. Dodge, Pres.
A. E. Duncan	H. W. Sherwood	William Stoddard
George W. Wright	L. J. Boyd	John A. Jones

THE DEACONS

CLASS OF 1943	CLASS OF 1944
Mrs. S. A. Dodge	Mrs. James Blair
Mrs. E. Broadbent	Mrs. George Wilson Vice-Moderator
Mrs. W. H. Campbell	
Mrs. Fred Woolfenden	Mrs. Robert Church
Mrs. W. E. Richardson	Mrs. John Fraser
	Mrs. A. E. Duncan

CLASS OF 1945

Mrs. A. Z. Cary
Mrs. E. Fairbairn
Mrs. George Hedges
Mrs. V. E. Palmer
Mrs. Paul Spielvogel
Mrs. John Inglis

THE CHURCH SCHOOL OF RELIGION

The Rev. James W. MacElree, General Superintendent

Charles Pennington, Ass't Sup't.　　E. C. Manns, Treasurer
Gordon Van Schaack, Int. Sup't.　　Mrs. Paul Pitzer, Exec. Sec.
Charles Pennington, Jr. Sup't.　　Robert Tennant, General Sec.
Janet Gulland, Ass't. Gen. Sec.　　Jean Hall, Enrollment Sec.

Beginners' Superintendents　　Primary Superintendents
Mrs. E. J. Outley　　Miss Ruth Dewers
Ruth Arnot　　Eleanor Garter

THE JUNIOR CHURCH

Mrs. A. E. Duncan　　　　Jean Hall

THE WOMAN'S UNION
President, Mrs. John N. Thomas

CIRCLE LEADERS

Naomi　　　　　　　　　Miriam
Mrs. Paul Pitzer　　　　　Mrs. A. B. McColl
Mary　　　　　　　　　　Vashti
Mrs. Harry Broadbent　　Mrs. E. C. Manns
Dorcas-Esther　　　　　　Martha
Mrs. J. W. Dammann　　Mrs. D. L. Edmiston
　　　　　Ruth
　　Mrs. H. M. Halvorsen

THE CHURCH ORGANIZATIONS

THE YOUNG PEOPLES C. E.................President, Donald Schulz
　　　　　　　　　　　　　　　　　Sponsor, Charles Pennington
THE JEAN SUTHERLAND GUILD...............Mrs. Gladys Jenkin
THE MOTHER'S CLUB........................Mrs. Thomas Garland
THE CLEOPHAS CLUB..................President, W. E. Richardson
THE HI-CLUB........................President, Jearold Cook
　　　　　　　　Sponsors, Mr. and Mrs. Russell Armstrong
SCOUT TROOP 6......................Chairman, Charles E. Bishop
　　　　　　　　　　　　　　　　　Scout Master, John Muns

SCOUT TROOP 90..Scout Master, Edgar S. Sells
GIRLS SCOUT TROOP 10......Scout Captain, Mrs. C. L. Hayward
CUB TROOP 6...Cubmaster, James Y. Harper
CAMP FIRE..Guardian, Mrs. Roger Barnes
HORIZON CLUB...Mrs. F. Feeley
CHURCH HISTORIAN...William Downie
COUNCIL OF CHURCHES REPRESENTATIVE....................
....Dr. John W. Hoffman

When Dr. Bechtel was planning to hold the 64th anniversary of Calvary Church in 1932, he realized that the historical records, including pictures of past officers and workers had, as before stated, been nearly all destroyed in the fire which had previously occurred. Therefore to somewhat remedy this condition the present writer was asked by Dr. Bechtel to do what he could in the way of reproducing part of the past history and pictures of its ex-officers over the past sixty-four years of its history. This the writer knew was an enormous task but then how could a fellow, with any heart, turn down a request from Dr. Bechtel? So the writer did his best, explaining to the merchants in the vicinity what we wished to accomplish, viz—the upholding of the Christian Church and its prestige in the community. To this the business men responded liberally (agreeing with us that moral dividends in any community are indispensable) and they made the bound history of 1932 not only self paying but able also to show a profit of $35.00 toward the building fund. In return for this generous help from the business men of the community we awarded each one a small amount of advertising space in the book. Several members of the congregation contributed toward the expense of the book and a large number of the books were sold.

WHERE PLACED ON FILE

These books were placed on file in several places and the reaction of each of these institutions follows some distance ahead, as well as some other historical matters of interest.

REPORT OF WILLIAM DOWNIE, APRIL 1st, 1934
ON HISTORY OF CALVARY CHURCH

To the Trustees and Elders of Calvary Church:

Three years ago Dr. Bechtel was appealing in the Bulletin for pictures of the early officers of the Church, such as the first pastor Dr. Atterbury, Rev. William Grandy, the second pastor, and Walter P. Kellogg, the first Sunday School Superintendent. A year later, in 1932, he was making an appeal for the same pictures, but again with no results. This kindled in the writer a determination to see what he could do. It will be remembered that the fire in 1916 had destroyed all of Calvary's records, so that in the year 1932, Calvary Church had no up-to-date account of her achievements, and almost no pictures of the men and women who, during the past 64 years had made Calvary one of the leading churches in Detroit. So with the idea of accomplishing what we lacked the writer started to work with the following results, upon the request of Dr. Bechtel.

We now have a complete history from the begnning, 1868, to the present time, including, First: Pictures of all the pastors of the church and the history of each one, including a picture of the wife of each pastor.

Second, Pictures and history of all of the 1st Board of Trustees.

Third, Pictures and history of the early Elders.

Fourth, Photostatic copy of the original Articles of Association, including history of each signer.

Fifth, A picture and history of the first Sunday School Superintendent and also of the second superintendent H. Kirke White former President of the D. M. Ferry Seed Co., and a list of every superintendent since.

Sixth, Many ancient documents, including a press report in 1869, of the dedication of the first Church, at Maybury Avenue and Butternut street, the dedication, in 1888, of the Michigan Avenue Church, the life and legal career of John G. Atterbury and his personal letters, in the year 1839, 30 years before Calvary Mission was formed, picture of the house in which Dr. Sutherland was born, photostatic copy of his marriage license, a picture of his father's blacksmith shop and many other documents of historical interest. All of the above I have compiled into two books, known as Book No. One and Book No. Two. Book No. One is to be in the continual custody of the pastor, not to be loaned outside of the church building, but may be examined by any one in the church edifice. Book No. Two is in the Burton Historical Library. In this way if one book should be be destroyed by fire, the duplicate history would still be available.

You may be curious to know how the writer has accomplished all this. It has been done by First: Tracing names in the City Directory as far back as 85 years; Second, An endless number of telephone calls and personal visits throughout the city and State; Third, A dragnet of letters of inquiry sent all over the United States to churches where our former pastors had preached, and from which they had been buried, asking the present pastor to appeal from the pulpit for a thorough search throughout the congregation for certain pictures; Fourth, A similar search, through the mail, of Probate Courts for records of heirs, cemeteries for records of relatives, County Treasurers for records of persons paying taxes, undertakers for names of remaining relatives, postmasters, public libraries for death notices in old newspaper files in their possession, health departments in other cities for death records, searching of city directories in other cities, and, in fact, a bombardment of letters running down every clue that could be found anywhere in any part of the United States. This meant the writing by the writer of over 100 letters in long hand and many more type written ones.

My work is now complete, simply awaiting the finishing of some typewritten matter.

There are some who have no appetite for this kind of work and perhaps would regard it as of little value, however, I will let the decision rest with the authors of the following five letters, which I hereby produce, the writers of which are experts in this line of work. I consider it a high honor to have received these letters from such distinguished authors and this honor I gladly share with Calvary Church.

Respectfully submitted,

Wm. Downie.

March 24, 1934. Continued.

LETTER FROM MR. GEORGE B. CATLIN, HISTORICAL WRITER OF THE DETROIT NEWS

Mr. William Downie,   Detroit, November 30, 1932.
4447 Vancouver Avenue,
Detroit, Michigan.

Dear Sir:

As a newspaper man and student of History, I rejoice to see the members of the Older churches of Detroit compiling the histories of these institutions in permanent form for the old generations are passing and the newer members are not so well informed with regard to the stories of their churches and the personality of the men who made them influential in the neighborhoods where they were located. Many thanks for the pamphlet on Founder's Day Celebration of Calvary Presbyterian Church. A copy should be sent to the Burton Historical Collection at the Public Library for a permanent record.

                 Appreciatively yours,
    Copy   George B. Catlin.
Writer's Note: (recently deceased).

Two copies are at the Burton Historical Library and a copy of this history of 1943 will also be sent there.

OFFICE OF THE GENERAL ASSEMBLY
DEPARTMENT OF HISTORY
THE PRESBYTERIAN HISTORICAL SOCIETY

520 Witherspoon Building
                 Philadelphia, June 15, 1932.

Rev. Leslie A. Bechtel, D.D.,
Detroit, Michigan.

We have received your exceptionally fine booklet, setting forth the Sixty-fourth Anniversary Celebration of the organization of Calvary Presbyterian Sunday School in Detroit with its wealth of historical material for which a grateful acknowledgment is hereby tendered.

       Copy   Your very truly,
Writer's Note: William P. Sinney, Secretary.

A copy will also be sent here of this history.

STATE OF MCHIGAN
MICHIGAN HISTORICAL COMMISSION
STATE OFFICE BUILDING
LANSING

Mr. William Downie,   December 7, 1932.
4447 Vancouver Avenue.
Detroit, Michigan.

Dear Mr. Downie:

    Many thanks for the copy of the History of the Calvary Presbyterian Church, which we are pleased to place in our files for future reference.

Very respectfully yours,
G. M. Fuller,
Secretary and Editor.

Copy

Writer's Note:

    A copy will also be sent here of this history.

THE BURTON HISTORICAL COLLECTION
OF THE PUBLIC LIBRARY
DETROIT, MICHIGAN

Sept. 29, 1932.

Mr. William Downie,
4447 Vancouver Avenue,
Detroit, Michigan.

Dear Sir:

    Your gift of two copies of the History of Calvary Presbyterian Church, which, you wrote in connection with the Founder's Day Celebration last June, is acknowledged with high appreciation. It is such carefully compiled personal accounts that place on record the work of men and women whose lives, though quiet, are more or less active as they endeavor to carry forward in their day and generation the task of the Kingdom.

Very truly yours,
G. B. Krum, Chief Librarian.

Writer's Note:

    A copy will also be sent here of this history.

PRESBYTERIAN BOARD OF CHURCH EXTENSION
THE PRESBYTERY OF DETROIT
Office 1109 Kresge Building

November 17, 1932.

Mr. William Downie,
4447 Vancouver Avenue,
Detroit, Michigan.

My dear Mr. Downie:

This letter will acknowledge receipt of the Founder's Day Celebration Booklet, containing the history of Calvary Presbyterian Church. We shall place it in our File for future reference. It is certainly well put together and has proven to be interesting reading as well as being of historical value.

Very sincerely yours,

Copy   M. C. PEARSON,
Writer's Note   Secy. and Treasurer.

A copy will also be sent here of this history.

FROM DETROIT NEWS, OCTOBER 15th, 1932
CHURCH BUILDS MEMORIAL UNIT
CORNERSTONE OF SUTHERLAND SUNDAY SCHOOL TO BE LAID TOMORROW

The cornerstone of the Sutherland Memorial Building of the Calvary Presbyterian Church will be laid Sunday morning at 10:30 o'clock.

The building, erected as a memorial to the late Dr. D. I. Sutherland, pastor of the church for 30 years, will have accommodations for a Sunday School of 1000 students. It was anticipated by Dr. Sutherland, who died before the project could be started.

The cornerstone will be laid by L. J. Armstrong. Assisting in the ceremonies will be B. F. Matthews, representing the session of the church; Geo. H. Willett representing the trustees; Vincent C. Palmer, chairman of the Board of Deacons, and Mrs. James Blair representing the Women's association, as well as by Miss Olive Sutherland, daughter, and the three grandchildren of Dr. Sutherland.

The cut showing the laying of the cornerstone is on page 57. No. 1 is Dr. L. A. Bechtel, No. 2 is L. J. Armstrong, No. 3 is Olive M. Sutherland, daughter of Dr. Sutherland. No. 4 is Jean Sutherland, No. 5 is David Sutherland, No. 6 is John Sutherland, No. 7 is B. F. Matthews, clerk of Session. No. 5, No. 6 and No. 4 are grandchildren of Dr. Sutherland. List of articles placed in the copper box of the cornerstone laid October 16th, 1932, in the Sutherland Memorial: 1. History of Calvary Church. 2. Copy of Detroit Free Press, Oct. 15th, 1932. 3. Picture of breaking of ground for Sutherland Memorial June 12, 1932. 4. Plans of the D. I. Sutherland Memorial. 5. Miscellaneous Church bulletins and papers. 6. Package of hollyhock seeds to be planted as an experiment at some distant date when the above copper box is opened. This box is hermetically sealed and it may form a very interesting experiment when, after a period of years, this box is opened and the seeds are planted, to see whether they will retain their life over such a span of years. Newspaper accounts show that seeds encased for several thousand years in Egyptian tombs sealed from the air sprouted when planted.

The original cost of the above first unit was $20,354.32 but to this could legitimately be added large sums since added in the way of equipment. Twelve thousand dollars worth of bonds were issued by the congregation, sold and redeemed in full by the church. The writer, Dr. Hoffman and Mr. John Sandick were the committee representing the bond holders and the committee has been discharged.

DEDICATING BOY SCOUT ROOM

During the last week of October, 1933, the women of the church served dinner dedicating the Boy Scout Room, and the whole new building through the first floor was turned over to the trustees the same week. Mr. John Sandick and the men of the church continued with much free service in finishing many of the details of the Scout Room, which otherwise would have been legitimate charges of the contractors against the trustees. Mr. John Gray, who with his family had been members of the church since the days of the little portable wooden chapel contributed several hundred dollars worth of electrical work free to the church. And so here in Calvary Church was produced (with its walls of natural wooden slabs) one of the finest and most quaint Boy Scout Rooms in America. It was conceived in the fertile mind of Dr. Bechtel and is a wonderful asset to Calvary Church. It is no wonder that the Scout movement flourishes here as well as all the other youth activities with such a home and environment to receive them.

FIRST FLOOR OF SUTHERLAND MEMORIAL

The first floor consists principally of Atterbury Chapel, Hall, Primary Room, Church office, two class rooms, Assistant Pastors' office and storage room for safe.

GOING BACK

In the year 1855 my father built and occupied a house at No. 366 Baker Street, now called Bagley Ave. He lived here for a few years and then moved to another part of the city. He rented the house to James Rankin, the first elder of Calvary Church, who was living in the house in the year 1868. It was perhaps about a fifteen minute walk from Calvary Mission. In the year 1935 the writer was still interested in this house and decided to tear it down. From the second story he delivered a joist to the home of Mr. John Sandick, one of our old time elders recently deceased and known to most all of the congregation. For the writer Mr. Sandick made a wall case with glass front to hang in the minister's study for the safe keeping of old Calvary relics. Among these relics you will see two gavels made also from the above joist and also two gavels made from a spindle of the stairway taken from the frame church at the southeast corner of Maybury and Butternut Streets and donated by the Dendel family. It contains also a gavel donated by Robert McKinnell, consisting of four pieces of wood, as follows: The mallet is made from dark oak taken from the Westminster Presbyterian Church, which was located on Washington Boulevard near State Street, sold to St. Aloysius Church, later torn down and replaced by the present newer St. Aloysius Church. Also wood (light oak) from the second Calvary Church, which was located on Michigan Ave. at Maybury—the handle is made of dark oak taken from the second Westminster edifice, which was located at the corner of Woodward Avnue and Parson Street, and also from white pine from the first Calvary Presbyterian Church, which was located at the southeast corner of Maybury Avenue and Butternut Street.

A TRIBUTE TO ROBERT McKINNELL

The Session of Calvary Church hereby individually express their deep sorrow at the passing of Robert McKinnell, who for many years was an exceptionally active worker in the affairs of Calvary Church.

The writer became acquainted with Mr. McKinnell on the evening of October 12th, 1912, this date being the 12th anniversary of the pastorate of the late Dr. D. I. Sutherland in the Michigan Ave. Church at Maybury Ave. For this occasion Mr. McKinnell wrote a historical sketch of the church, which is now included in Calvary's official scrap book, securely locked in the church vault.

Mr. McKinnell's father located in the neighborhood of Calvary Church on Michigan Ave. away back in the 70's, after arriving from England, where Robert was born. In the year 1879 young Robert joined Calvary Sunday School when Rev. Wm. Grandy (noted for his heroic work with the tornado victims of 1875) was pastor.

Perusing the records of Calvary Church, we find that Mr. McKinnell was an exceptionally active member in guiding the affairs of the Church for a period of about thirty-five years. He served as Elder, Trustee, Sunday School Superintendent, Clerk of Session, and was appointed Commissioner Sept. 13th, 1900, to inform the Presbytery meeting at Brighton, Michigan, of the call to Dr. Sutherland from Calvary Church. He was very active in the social affairs of the Church. He contributed innumerable interesting relics which he had collected from over a period of years (bulletins, newspapers, pictures, etc.), depicting past events of long ago in the early life of Calvary Church.

As a fore-runner of Calvary Church in its present location, he held Sunday Morning Services in his own home on Oregon Avenue, near Grand River Ave. This was just previous to the erection of the little portable Chapel preceding the present edifice about the year 1914.

His interest and activity in Calvary Church were intense but about this time he moved to another part of the city and became affiliated with the Woodward Church nearer to his home. But he never lost interest in Calvary, his first love. I do not believe that any re-union has since been held in Calvary Church that the assemblage has not been graced by the familiar, welcome presence of Robert McKinnell.

And so, in appreciation of his splendid work in Calvary Church, it is hereby ordered by the session of this church that:

To you, dear Mrs. McKinnell, this memoir be sent with the deep sympathy of the members of this church and with the earnest hope that this record of Mr. McKinnell's fine religious activities in this church will somewhat comfort you in your present great sorrow. And it is further ordered by the session that a copy be included in the minutes of this board and another copy preserved in the historical records of the church.

Most sincerely yours,
SESSION OF CALVARY PRESBYTERIAN CHURCH,
By Leslie A. Bechtel,
Dated Jan. 15th, 1942.   Pastor.
S. A. Dodge,
Clerk of Session.
William Downie.

Detroit Public Schools
CASS TECHNICAL HIGH SCHOOL
2421 Second Boulevard
Detroit, Michigan.

December 16, 1932.

Mr. William Downie,
4447 Vancouver Avenue,
Detroit, Michigan.

My dear Mr. Downie:

Your request for my experience as a member of the infant class in Calvary Mission Sunday School in 1869 at Maybury Grand Avenue and Butternut Street, Detroit, Michigan has pleased me very much. To be able after three score and four years to bear testimony to the heroic and religious spirit of those who labored in God's Kingdom to found Calvary Presbyterian Church is indeed a great privilege.

My first religious awakening was as a child in Calvary infant class with Mary and Elizabeth Maltz as my teachers. I was but five years old and well can I remember at this day how Elizabeth used to play the small organ and Mary used to stand before us children and teach us to sing:

"Jesus loves me, this I know
For the Bible tells me so."

They were noble young women, members of the Westminster Presbyterian Church, Washington Boulevard and State Street, now St. Aloysius Roman Catholic Church. Rev. W. E. McLaren was the minister of this Church when the Sunday School was first organized. I remember him and the Superintendent, Mr. Kellogg, very well. The Rev. Mr. McLaren was a tall man with handsome features, and I remember that he wore Galway side whiskers. He resigned as pastor of Westminster Church to accept a call to an Episcopalian Church in Chicago and soon afterward was elevated to the Episcopate of the Diocese of Illinois. He was a very eloquent preacher indeed.

The Calvary Mission Sunday School was a great boon to all of the good people of the west end of Detroit in those days. It was established soon after the Civil War; money—"greenbacks"— was plentiful and a great boom of building was going on in this section and the Sunday School prospered. The frame building at the corner of Maybury Grand Avenue and Butternut used to be filled every Sunday. The infant class was in the rear and was separated from the main auditorium by sliding glass partitions which could be raised when the whole school was conducted by the Superintendent, Mr. Kellogg, in a general exercise of song and prayer. Indeed, there were many inspiring meetings in this primitive temple devoted to religious education, especially when the annual Christmas tree exercises were held. The Mission Church would be packed to overflowing on these occasions and every child would receive a gift from the tree, also a stocking of candy and pop-corn ball. I well recall on one occasion, I was called up like all the others and my name, Benny Comfort, was announced, I went up to the tree with great expectations. Mr. Kellogg gave me a rooster with a whistle on it, and of course my bag of candy and pop-corn ball, which I took with much joy, but when I came down the aisle to my mother and father, I blew the whistle with great gusto and the whole audience laughed and applauded at my glee.

The Presbyterian Churches of the whole city contributed money and teachers to Calvary Mission and none of those who faithfully contributed their time and talents to this good work did more than Mary and Elizabeth Maltz. For years they conducted the infant class in the Mission and also collected money and groceries and clothes to relieve distress among the poor and unfortunate on the west side. They were good angels to many families who needed assistance in their misery and misfortune.

But I must not forget to relate the romantic side of this mission work of these two young women, Mary and Elizabeth Maltz. At the time the Mission started in 1869, my father had returned from his position during the Civil War and after, from 1860 to 1869, as Special Indian Agent at L'Anse, Michigan, among the Chippewa Indians. He resumed his house-building business and settled in a home on Michigan Avenue at the head of 20th Street. At this point was the terminal, then, of the horse cars of the time and the beginning of the plank road which went out the Chicago highway to Jackson and Chicago—now Michigan Avenue. As the cars ran only at long intervals, the Comfort cottage became the headquarters, on cold and bitter winter days, of the mission people who came from downtown on the street cars. Among those who were in this group, of course, were Mary and Elizabeth Maltz. Many times on their journeys out to the Mission they would stop at our house and my mother always had a hot cup of tea and other refreshments for them. They became fast friends of the family, and although I was but five years old when they first came, I became quite attached to both of them, for they were my teachers. However, I remember that on these visits there was a young man who nearly always accompanied them on Sundays, whose name was Robert S. Bowring. My only brother, who was nineteen at that time, became acquainted with these missionaries and Mr. Bowring and used to go with them to Sunday School. In the due course of time Mary became Mrs. Robert S. Bowring and Elizabeth became Mrs. John C. Comfort, my sister-in-law.

Mr. and Mrs. Robert S. Bowring lived in Detroit many years and conducted a millinery business on Bates Street at the head of Fort Street East, and about 1884 went out to Spokane and met business reverses, whereupon they returned to Chicago, where Mr. Bowring was employed in a large wholesale shoe house. They lived happily together in Chicago for many years, when Mrs. Bowring died about 1916. They had no children. Mr. Bowring is still alive.

Mr. and Mrs. John C. Comfort were married in Detroit in 1873, and soon after their marriage went to Alpena, Michigan, where Mr. Comfort served as Cashier of the Alpena National Bank for forty years, and in 1914 retired and went to Chicago, where Mrs. Comfort could be near Mr. and Mrs. Bowring in their declining years.

Mrs. Comfort died in Chicago in 1924 and Mr. Comfort died in San Antonio, Texas, in 1929. They are both buried in Woodmere Cemetery, Detroit.

The children surviving their union are George Newell Comfort of Cleveland, Ohio; Robert Bowring Comfort of Chicago, Illinois, and Mary Bowring Comfort Stepler of Chicago, Illinois.

BENJ. F. COMFORT,
Principal, Cass Technical High School,
Detroit, Michigan.

Mr. Comfort left his earthly abode about the year 1941.

Reminiscence in 1932 of Mrs. Agnes Telfer Boothroyd of the cottage mission on Michigan Avenue near 23rd Street in 1868 and also the Butternut Street Church at the very beginning, 1869:

To the dear members of Calvary Presbyterian Church, the church in which I was born and raised, the church which holds for me so many tender memories and the church that I love:

I have lived my whole lifetime practically in my present home at 2106 20th Street. I attended the cottage mission. We entered by a side door. The front portion was rented for a meat market. The officers had tried out a location on Harrison Avenue in 1868 but decided to found the mission on Michigan Avenue, believing this to be the better of the two sections.

My home has been the scene of many happy meetings with all of the early officers and workers. Walter P. Kellogg, the first superintendent, and Charles A. King were business partners. Mr. Kellogg left Detroit for Denver, Colo., about 1890.

Peter Young was a commission merchant. Each year he chartered a boat and took the Sunday School to Slocum's Island. The teachers provided free lunches, lemonade and street car transportation to and from the boat.

Two sisters, Mary and Elizabeth Maltz, had charge of the Primary Department. Mary Maltz married Robert S. Bowring, and Elizabeth Maltz married John Comfort—banker of Alpena, Michigan—and brother of Benjamin F. Comfort, present principal of Cass Technical High School.

Mr. H. Kirke White came out and taught. He was connected with the D. M. Ferry Seed Company.

Levi P. Griffin, a very noted attorney of Detroit and a member of Congress, also came out and taught.

Some of the other teachers that I recall were: Mrs. Zug, who with her husband owned Zug Island in the Rouge River: Miss Ayers, Miss C. McMillan, Mrs. Shotwell, Miss Aikman, Grace and Annie Rankin, Mr. Brownell, John Comfort, Mr. O. W. Gulley, Mr. Peter Voorheis and still some others that I cannot recall.

We, as youngsters, waited longingly for each Friday night to roll around, when dear old Dr. Atterbury would come first to our house and from here we would all go up to the Friday evening prayer meeting in the Butternut Street Church. He loved children. Loved to tell them stories and we all loved him.

These first teachers in the mission were nearly all from the Westminster Church and came from downtown each Sunday to teach. At that time Westminster Church occupied the present site of the St. Aloysius Catholic Church on Washington Blvd.

Then I have happy remembrances of Bradford Smith, the whole Rankin family, the Plumers, Osbornes, Gentles and Reids, the Shotwells, the Davis family, the Cheney family and many others.

Nettie Plumer, now Mrs. Wm. H. Blackford, too small to go alone, came hand in hand with her big brother, John Plumer, to the Michigan Avenue cottage mission.

I was intimately acquainted with all the signers of the original Articles of Association.

I knew intimately Rev. W. E. McLaren, the first Westminster pastor in our cottage mission. He was a lovely man, very fond of children. Later he became Bishop of the Episcopal Church for the State of Illinois. He was followed by Rev. Wm. Aikman in Westminster Church. Miss Aikman also taught in our mission.

Many, many happy days I have spent in old Calvary Church and many are the happy memories that I retain. Distance prevents me from attending oftener than I do but I come when I can. My heart is still in Calvary Church and my best wishes are for her and her pastor, Dr. Bechtel, and I'll just close by saying—may God continue to bless dear old Calvary.

(Singed)   AGNES TELFER BOOTHROYD,
2106 20th Street, Detroit, Michigan.
Date. December 19th, 1932.

Mrs. Boothroyd died about 1939.

SEVENTIETH ANNIVERSARY OF CALVARY PRESBYTERIAN CHURCH AND SUNDAY SCHOOL.

Friday Evening, October 7th, 1938.

Another glorious day in the history of Calvary Church under Dr. Bechtel.

The following program was presented. As will be seen, we had as one of our guest speakers on the programme that master of economic logic, Mr. Wm. J. Cameron of the Ford Motor Co., whose talk was most entertaining and educational, and a musical programme presented by the Beta Chapter of the Delta Omicron National Music Sorority.

PROGRAMME

1. Community Singing..................Songs of Bygone Days
       Mr. Orville Coppock   Mr. Ross Nelson
2. Address of Welcome....................Dr. Lesie A. Bechtel
3. "How It All Came About"..........Chairman William Downie
4. Selections ....String Ensemble
5. a. The Wild Rose ....Dvorak
   b. The Fugitive ....Dvorak
      Dorothy Buchbinder, Soprano. Frances Bremer, Contralto
6. Greetings from Our Superintendent..Mr. Lawrence W. Downie
7. Two Minute Greetings from Ex-Superintendents.

8. a. Londonderry Air ....Arr. Kreisler
   b. Waltz .... Brahms
   c. Shoenrosmarin .... Kreisler
                    Doris Yoder, Violinist
9. a. A Birthday ....Woodman
   b. Carmena .... Wilson
                  Helen Downie Bishop, Soprano
10. Selection ....String Ensemble
11. Address of the Evening.......................Mr. William J. Cameron
                                       of the Ford Motor Co.

    We particularly welcome Mr. Wm. J. Cameron on our programme tonight, because as a boy he attended the old Calvary Sunday School.

12. "Auld Lang Syne"..Entire Audience

    The Musical Program is presented by the Beta Chapter of the Delta Omicron National Music Sorority. Accompanist, Marie Marti.

    To the supper and programme were also invited Mr. E. J. Wheatley and family of Detroit. Mr. Wheatley is the artist who painted in oil the beautiful picture 4 feet by 12 feet long, depicting Calvary as a lighthouse lighting the way for the world and guiding the ship safely into the harbor. The painting adjoins the gallery on the Grand' River end of the church and has been appraised at a value of seven hundred dollars by an art dealer. With Mr. Wheatley it was a labor of love and friendship to Calvary Presbyterian Church, to whom he donated it at the request of the author.

    The address that the programme showed should have been delivered by Mr. Lawrence W. Downie as Sunday School Superintendent was not given, as he was unavoidably detained in England and sent the following cablegram:

Calvary Church—Grand River and Vicksburg Avenues,
Detroit, Michigan.

    "Congratulations seventieth anniversary. Regret we cannot be with you. Hope you have most enoyable evening. Am looking forward to a splendid school year. Anticipate returning soon. Best wishes to all."

                                  LAWRENCE DOWNIE.

DR. BECHTEL ELECTED MODERATOR

On April 18th, 1939, Dr. Bechtel was elected at Monroe, Michigan, in the First Presbyterian Church of that place to be moderator of the Detroit Presbytery.

FROM THE DETROIT POST, MONDAY, DECEMBER 13, 1869.
SUNDAY SERVICES
DEDICATION OF CALVARY MISSION CHAPEL

Yesterday afternoon at 3 o'clock, Calvary Mission Chapel, on Maybury Avenue, near Michigan Avenue, was dedicated. Thus is added another to the list of houses of Christian worship which have sprung up in the rapidly growing outskirts of the city. The building has already been described in these columns. It is a neat and substantial wooden chapel, capable of comfortably seating 500 children. The interior is divided into three compartments, so arranged that all can be thrown into one whenever occasion requires. The largest of these rooms is designed for the general audience room. The others are Bible and infant class rooms. The building was erected at a cost of $4,000, of which sum $3,000 was considered as provided for. This, however, included a mortgage of $1,000, which is expected to be liquidated without delay. The balance, $1,000, unprovided for, was raised by subscription during the dedicatory exercises yesterday. The lot was donated by Mr. Bradford Smith.

The chapel is admirably located, being in an already thickly settled and rapidly growing neighborhood, far away from a church of any kind. Maybury Avenue (Twenty-second Street) has been but recently opened, and extends from Michigan Avenue to Grand River Avenue. Though the lots were put on the market but a few months ago, there are already probably fifty or more houses on the street. Michigan Avenue and other streets in the vicinity are quite thickly built up, and the neighborhood may fairly be called populous. Those who have not lately been out on Michigan Avenue to the Junction will be surprised to see the rapid growth and the improvements which the past summer has wrought. With this material advancement goes the spirit which builds, in the midst of the shops and new made dwellings, the house of Christian worship.

The chapel was crowded yesterday by children of the neighborhood and by patrons and friends of the enterprise, who had gone thither to participate in the dedicatory exercises. After prayer by the Rev. Mr. McCorkle, and singing, Mr. Walter P. Kellogg, Superintendent of the Mission School, gave a brief history of the enterprise. He said that a year ago last May a few young men in Westminster Church met together and determined to start a Mission Sabbath School. They first secured a little room over a grocery store on Harrison Avenue, where they opened their school. The first Sunday they had four or five teachers and just two scholars with perhaps half a dozen hanging curiously about. The next Sunday there were a dozen scholars, and the number continued to increase. During the summer the attendance averaged 30. The place soon proved too small to meet the requirements, and in casting about for new quarters it was determined to go toward the outskirts of the city. The present location was determined upon as being a place destitute of religious privileges. A little cottage was secured, and a year ago last October the school was opened with 50 scholars. The number continued to increase until, in a short time, there were 160 scholars. Then it was found that the cottage was too small, and it was determined to build this chapel. The friends of the enterprise came forward liberally and the building was soon erected, and this is the glad day of its dedication, and it is indeed a glad day for those whom God has raised up for building this house. There are now about 15 teachers in the school, and the names of 250 children on the rolls. It is expected that the number of children will be increased to 400 or 500 within a few weeks. More teachers are needed.

Remarks appropriate to the occasion were made by the Rev. Dr. Hogarth, pastor of the Jefferson Avenue Presbyterian Church; the Rev. Mr. Pierson, pastor of the Fort Street Presbyterian Church; the Rev. Dr. McKown, President of Albion College; Mr. Bradford Smith, the Rev. Mr. Lyon of Detroit; the Rev. W. E. McLaren, pastor of the Westminster Presbyterian Church, and by others. The exercises were agreeably interspersed with singing by the school, and proved to be of a very entertaining and profitable character.

CALVARY'S SEVENTY-FIVE YEARS

FROM THE DETROIT FREE PRESS, TUESDAY, MAY 31, 1887

PERSEVERING PRESBYTERIANS

The Corner Stone of the New Calvary Church Laid in a Downpour of Rain

The Stone the Gift of the Primary Classes of the Sabbath School

At 2:30 o'clock yesterday afternoon, the hour named for the laying of the corner stone of the new Calvary Presbyterian Church, at the corner of Michigan and Maybury avenues, the clouds were gray and the rain fell in a steady, dreary drizzle, varied by occasional vicious dashes, heavier, but scarcely more dispiriting.

The disagreeable weather did not, however, prevent the gathering of a crowd sufficient to occupy every inch of standing room within hearing of the speakers, which remained patient and attentive under their upraised umbrellas for more than an hour and did not begin to scatter until after the stone had been lowered to its place, the rain began to fall in a blinding torrent.

The walls of the church have reached the level of the main floor, except at the place where a gap had been left for the stand, and the space to be occupied by the vestibule was floored, railed and supplied with chairs for the accommodation of clergymen, officers of the church and guests from other congregations. This platform was completely filled and the pavement of Michigan avenue was thronged to the car tracks, while the sidewalks and windows of buildings opposite were also crowded with those who, as they could not hear, were obliged to make the most of seeing.

Upon the platform reserved for the participants in the ceremonies, were the Revs. J. F. Dickie, D. M. Cooper, Wallace Radcliffe, Louis R. Fox, and George W. Barlow, pastor of the church, and Messrs. W. S. Crawford, H. K. White and Jacob S. Farrand, who have been among its most open handed friends.

The Michigan Central Band, stationed at the rear of the audience, after playing a variety of selections, opened the programme with an impressive rendition of "Nearer My God to Thee," after which Rev. J. F. Dickie offered a brief prayer, the audience attending, their bared heads bowing under the steadily falling rain.

The Rev. D. M. Cooper next read two very brief Scriptural selections, appropriate to the founding of the walls of the material church, after which the Rev. Dr. Wallace Radcliffe advanced and made the principal address of the day, which, with admirable consideration for those assembled in such trying weather, he made very brief. He said, in effect:

"The corner stone of this church is laid in the approved Presbyterian manner, with the ceremony of sprinkling. We may well, on such a day and for such a purpose, cheerfully endure some discomfort, for our ancestors, who founded and transmitted to us as a heritage the church which we love, feared neither rain nor tempest and met the fiercer assault of persecution with calmness and unflinching fortitude.

"This corner stone is laid upon the solid foundation of faith in the Lord Jesus Christ, and a steadfast continuance in the faith alone can insure the future to which the walls are reared. The church is not erected as merely a pleasant gathering place—a kind of social club for the congregation—but as a gathering place of true believers, banded together because they do believe in the Lord Jesus Christ, the son of God and of man, the only hope of sinful and suffering humanity.

"It is to be, too, not only a church of Christ, but a Presbyterian Church, for we do not forget that we are Presbyterians, nor are we ashamed of our name. Our church is not a narrowly-sectarian one, but is ever ready to join hands with all who are baptized in the name of Christ. We are not Presbyterians because we believe ours the only way to salvation, but because for us it is the best way. We rejoice in the polity of our church and are proud of its noble origin, its grand history and its present splendid unity; proud that it has always been foremost in the cause of everything that is pure and lowly and of good report, and we lay this cornerstone full of a proud faith in Christ, in the steadfastness of God's people and the future—the continuity for good.

"As this church rises the influences for evil about it must go down and in the community at large as well as to its immediate membership it cannot fail to prove a source of material as well as of moral and spiritual good."

The speaker closed by drawing a striking comparison between the two events of the day—the unveiling of a fountain destined to freely supply pure, cold water to thirsty generations and the laying of the corner stone of a church, from which shall flow a spiritual stream as pure, as refreshing and as free.

At the conclusion of Dr. Radcliffe's remarks the Rev. Mr. Barlow stated that the corner stone was paid for by the accumulated contributions of the primary classes of the Sabbath School, and that the children—placing their pennies, dimes and quarters with the dollars of their elders—had done more than their share toward the general building fund. Calvary Church, he said, is the outgrowth of a Sabbath school and the children—the hope of the church—still outnumber the grown members.

The primary classes then repeated some verses in unison, and sang, in their sweet, piping treble, "We are Little Laborers."

The pastor then called upon W. S. Crawford, whom he described as one of Calvary's best and most liberal friends, to place the usual sealed tin box in the corner-stone, which that gentleman did after a few words of acknowledgment and affectionate advice to the children. The stone was then lowered to its place without further ceremony.

The box contained a Bible; the hymnal used by the church; a copy of the church paper, The Chimes; a brief history of the church; a record of its last annual meeting, and a programme of the day.

A tremendous downpour began at this point, and the remaining exercises being hastily passed over, the assemblage was dismissed with the doxology and the benediction by the Rev. Louis R. Fox.

The church is of brick and will have a slate roof. It will be 100 feet long, the front, from the outer edges of the towers, measuring 74 feet. The height of the square tower will be 90 feet. From the ground to the point of the roof 65 feet. The auditorium will be 72x52 feet, besides gallery over the vestibule, and will comfortably seat 776 persons. It will be 18 feet high on the sides and 32 in the center. The roof trusses will be partly exposed, and the windows of stained glass. The first floor will seat 700 children easily. It will be arranged with sliding doors, forming a large lecture room or main Sabbath school room, and infant school room, a young people's Bible class room and a kitchen. All these rooms, except the kitchen, will be so open that every person in them is in full view of the platform. The furnaces will be in a room excavated under the first floor.

Writer's Note:

Mr. Warren E. Brinkerhoff who was the structural engineer of the Detroit Bridge and Iron Works witnessed across the fields from his office the whole laying of the corner stone. He was not a member of the church then but was its treasurer just prior to the building of the Grand River Church. Twenty-five years ago he confirmed to me this Free Press story of the rain during the laying of the corner stone.

INTO THE NEW CHURCH

From Free Press of Thursday, January 26th, 1888

Dedication Services of the Calvary Presbyterian Edifice

Perhaps the largest assembly of the members of the Calvary Presbyterian Church that ever came together was present last evening at the dedicatory exercises of the new edifice of the society, located at the corner of Maybury and Michigan avenues. For years the Calvary Church has occupied a building at the corner of Maybury avenue and Butternut street, the new building being but an ordinary evidence of the growth of a church society, with the exception that in this instance the growth has been somewhat phenomenal.

The present edifice faces Maybury avenue and is located on Michigan. It is 100 feet in length, built of brick and stone, with slate roof and has a frontage of 74 feet on Michigan avenue. Its height is 90 feet at the tower on the left front corner and the peak of the roof is 65 feet from the ground. The auditorium is 72x52 feet in size, with a gallery over the entrance, and will comfortably seat 700 people. The roof trusses are partly seen and are eighteen feet from the floor at the sides and thirty-two feet in the center. The auditorium is arranged in amphitheater form. The Sunday school room is enirely above ground and has seating capacity for 700 children, arranged in divisions, connected with each other by sliding doors. The corner-stone of the edifice was laid in May, 1887.

The exercises of the dedication were prayers, Scriptural reading by Rev. J. M. Barkley and addresses by Rev. Wallace Radcliffe, of the Fort Street Presbyterian Church, and by Rev. Howard Duffield, pastor of the Westminster Church. A choir, of members of the church, rendered a number of anthems. A number of other churches of the city were represented by their pastors, among whom were Revs. J. F. Dickie, of the Central; L. R. Fox, of the Union; Richard Turnbull, of the United; C. S. Eastman and S. P. Warner.

The Treasurer's report showed the cost of the new edifice, exclusive of the site, to have been $20,976. The cash received to the date of making the report was $13,200, and the church debt was said to be $7,976.28. The amount raised by the church was $8,400 besides the lot, and friends in the city had swelled the amount to $13,000. The stained glass windows of the building were furnished by the following individuals and societies of the church, each providing one: Choir, Ladies' Aid Society, Chautauqua Circle, "five cents" subscription, primary room, H. K. White; a window in commemoration of George Mead furnished by his father, Sunday school classes, cheerful givers, Young People's Bible Class, daughters of the circle, foreign missionary guild and memorials of the first pastors of the church and Rev. Dr. Atterbury. The pulpit was donated by an anonymous friend. With the $7,000 debt in mind the pastor of the church, Rev. George W. Barlow, arose, produced a blackboard, divided the debt into shares and sold $1,000 worth of shares in less than fifteen minutes.

Jacob S. Farrand, to whom credit is due for much of the success of the church, addressed the society and he succeeded in raising $500. Announcement was made that James McMillan and Mrs. John S. Newberry would each donate $500 to decrease the church debt. Altogether $3,181 was raised that night by pledges, being within a fraction of one-half of the debt pledged.

The present officers of the church are: George W. Barlow, Pastor. Elders George Roe, Charles T. Duffie, Wm. McKerrow, H. R. Ford, W. M. Caldwell; Clerk, John Munro; Trustees, Samuel A. Plumer, Chairman, John Mead, George Mead, Collector, Geo. W. Stringer; Treasurer, Edwin Bates, W. R. Montgomery; Secretary, John H. Craddock.

THESE ARE PHOTOSTATIC COPIES OF PAGES 348, 349, 350 351 OF BOOK C OF OLD RECORDS IN ROOM 516 WAYNE COUNTY BUILDING
ARTICLES OF ASSOCIATION OF THE
CALVARY CHURCH OF DETROIT

The undersigned being desirous of forming themselves into a religious society under the provisions of an act of the Legislature of the State of Michigan entitled "An act concerning churches and religious societies establishing uniform rules for the acquisition, tenure, control and disposition of property conveyed or dedicated for religious purposes and to repeal chapter fifty-two of the Revised Statutes. Approved February 13th, 1855, and acts amendatory thereto." Do hereby associate themselves together and adapt the following.

ARTICLES

1

The object of this association shall be to provide for he maintenance of public worship and the institution of religion in the Calvary Church of Detroit now attached to the Presbytery of Detroit and Synod of Michigan.

11

The affairs of this association shall be managed by six Trustees who shall be divided into three classes so that one-third part of the whole number of the Trustees may be annually chosen.

111

The name by which the said Trustees and their successors in office shall be known and called shall be the Calvary Church of Detroit.

Witness our hands this eighteenth day of November in the year one thousand eight hundred and seventy-two.

    Sylvanus Warren—retired minister
    James Rankin—brass founder
    Thos. McEwing—carpenter
    Abel Shotwell—grocer
    David Reid—cabinet maker
    John R. Gentle—architect and builder
    Benj. Neal—with Grinnell Bros. music house

John S. Rankin—timber surveyor
Bradford Smith—school teacher and realtor

Writer's note—The above were the occupations of the signers of the articles of association in 1872.

State of Michigan
County of Wayne
S.S.

We James Rankin sole Elder of Calvary Church of Detroit and Sylvanus Warren a voter and nominated by a majority of voters for inspector of the election herein set forth. Do hereby certify that a meeting composed of Sylvanus Warren, James Rankin, Thomas McEwing, Abel Shotwell, David Reid, John R. Gentle, Benjamin Neal and John S. Rankin and others, all of whom being persons who had signed articles of association for the purpose of forming themselves into a religious society under the Statutes of the State of Michigan in that case made and provided, was held in the chapel on the corner of Mayberry Avenue and Butternut Street in the City of Detroit, on the evening of Monday the eighteenth day of November in the year one thousand eight hundred and seventy-two in pursuance of the following notice, publicly read in the said chapel by the officiating clergyman, in the presence and during the public service of the congregation, known as the Calvary Church of Detroit, on the following Sabbath to wit: on the third, the tenth and the seventeenth days of November in the year aforesaid, namely "Notice is hereby given that a meeting will be held in this place on Monday evening the 18th day of November instant at half past seven o'clock for the purpose of electing, not less than three nor more than nine trustees to take charge of the property belonging to and to transact all affairs relating to the temporalities of this congregation.

And we do further certify that at the said meeting the following persons being laymen were duly elected by ballot to serve as said trustees, namely

Darwin D. Davis	John R. Gentle
Samuel A. Plumer	Albert Shotwell
David S. Osborn	Bradford Smith

And we do further certify that at said meeting the name by which the said Trustees and their successors in office shall be known and called was then and there declared to be "The Calvary Church of Detroit."

In witness whereof we have hereunto set our hands and seals this eighteenth day of November A.D. 1872.

James Rankin   Seal
Sylvanus Warren   Seal

State of Michigan
County of Wayne
S.S.

On this (23) twenty-third day of November in the year one thousand eight hundred and seventy-two, personally before me a notary public in and for the said County of Wayne appeared James Rankin and Sylvanus Warren the persons described in and who executed the foregoing certificate and acknowledged the same to be their act and deed

E. C. Walker,
Notary Public,
Wayne County, State of Michigan.
M. J. Moynahan,

Received for record filed and recorded this 9th day of December 1872.

Dept. Clerk.

Writer's Note:

Mr. Shotwell's name was Abel Shotwell as page 349 of the above articles shows a copy of the way he signed his name. Robert Reid who knew him very intimately says that his name was Abel. It will be seen that the name Albert Shotwell on page 350 is not a copy of his own hand writing but is obviously an error of the person who wrote the affidavit signed by James Rankin and Sylvanus Warren.

Note: The church was organized by a committee of Presbytery Oct. 3rd, 1872, and the above articles of association were signed November 18th, 1872, and recorded with county clerk December 9th, 1872. The mission however was started four years earlier in the spring of 1868,

THE ENTIRE D. I. SUTHERLAND MEMORIAL NOW COMPLETE

On December 3rd, 1939, John Sutherland, grandson of Dr. Sutherland, applied a match to a $12,000 mortgage which the church burned at that Sunday morning service. A campaign had been started the previous April which netted $20,000.

Leaving $8,000.00 to be applied on the second and final story, much praise is due Elder Harry Logan for his successful and energetic pushing of this campaign. This story will be called Memorial Hall. It contains a beautiful parlor called the Jean Sutherland room artistically furnished by Miss Olive Sutherland, the daughter, a long hall way, the Gray Room, the Plumer Room, Jenkin Room and the Hammond Room. In the center is Memorial Chapel and on the west side is the kitchenette. There are 24 windows in the second story of Sutherland Building each bearing its own memorial. The entire indebtedness on the real estate is now only $6,700, approximately covered by a mortgage at only 4% over an original period of ten years. So as has always been, Calvary is traveling conservatively and safely, her property at all times secure from foreclosure, due to the caution of her officers and assisted in their decisions by the conservative good judgment of our pastor, Dr. Bechtel. We are not a wealthy people but each member as a rule tries to do his part. Team work is what counts. And so we believe that we have one of the most practical church and Sunday School buildings in the State.

FLOWER DAY

Flower Day every May was suggested by Orville Coppock, director and organist. It has been carried out for several years. The idea is to take a bouquet to some friend in the church. It enriches the pulpit and makes the recipient happy. My only regret is that several worthy souls each year fail to receive one—just an oversight.

CANDLE LIGHT SERVICES

Candle light services have been inaugurated and held Christmas Eve and Good Friday by Dr. Bechtel for several years and have proved to be a very beautiful service. The auditorium has always been filled to overflowing.

MOTHER'S DAY

Mother's Day observance once a year has always been held in the auditorium with marked success including a good sermon appropriate for the occasion by the Pastor.

MOTHER AND DAUGHTER AND FATHER AND SON BANQUETS

These both have been held yearly in the gymnasium with excellent dinners provided at a reasonable price, followed by splendid programmes. Attendance is always large.

NEW UP TO DATE KITCHEN

Our main kitchen off the gymnasium is a model of beauty and utility. People always will differ in the precise manner of laying out a kitchen or any other room, but on the whole we have here an excellent piece of work and paid for by the Women's Union. The women of the church have worked wonderfully (hand in hand) at all times from the start of the church in 1868 down to the present time in keeping the finances of the organization in excellent shape.

ART WINDOWS IN BAD SHAPE

Through the ravishes of time and weather all of the art windows of 1887 in the main auditorium have shown the strain. At great expense they have recently been surrounded by permanent storm sash through which their beauty is still seen and which will prolong their endurance many years more.

MISSIONARY, CHARITY AND PHILANTHROPIC WORK

These have been carried out in abundance. No worthy call goes out for help anywhere in the congregation or elsewhere that does not meet with a quick sympathetic response. Everything of course is investigated.

S. A. DODGE MOVING PICTURES

Mr. Dodge, our church secretary and president of the Board of Trustees, has a very fine moving picture machine and has taken several reels which will be interesting to see when he places them on display as time goes on.

WELFARE BASKETS

The Women's Union through their committee for many years has sent a liberal basket to many needy people at both Thanksgiving and Christmas. Mr. Burt Hammond, Ex-trustee and Elder, for several years, at his own personal expense, has worked in a chicken into each basket. In addition to the above the Kolah Club and other organizations have not failed to gladden the hearts and stomachs of many needy families.

REPORT OF RED CROSS BY MRS. ROBERT E. GOWANS, SECRETARY

The Calvary Presbyterian Church Unit of the American Red Cross was organized in June, 1940, and began work on the tenth day of that month. Through February 28th, 1943, more than 680 members have been registered with the unit in the three types of work, (knitting, sewing, and the making of surgical dressings), and a grand total of 88,244 hours has been credited to them.

At this time surgical dressings by the thousands are being made each day as there is a large quota to be met. An average of 100 surgical workers meet in the Memorial Chapel of the church each Tuesday from 10:00 A.M. to 3:00 P.M., and in the last seven months they have made 97,838 dressings. The sewing machines are set up in one of the small rooms just off the Memorial Chapel, and here a group of between fifteen and twenty women have made 3,510 garments, as well as 146 complete layettes, 91 pieced baby quilts, and 43 defense laprobes. The knitters number about 100, and they have made 2,195 garments, and 21 afghans.

Several members of the unit spend each Tuesday morning preparing a snack luncheon of sandwiches, beverage, and dessert, and this is served buffet style at a nominal charge to the Red Cross workers.

Officers of the unit are:
Mrs. W. E. Richardson, Chairman
Mrs. F. S. Balnaves, Vice-Chairman
Mrs. Robert S. Gowans, Secretary
Mrs. John J. Fraser, Treasurer

SOME THINGS OUR EARLY MINISTERS SAW

But those sights have gone from the scene forever.

Dr. Atterbury had been back from New York City just about three years when as a small boy about three years of age, I awakened one Sunday morning just before daylight finding myself between my father and mother. My mother also had awakened. It was winter. Snow covered the ground. "Mother," said I, "what is that noise I hear?" "Son," said she, "that is the city lamp man making the rounds to put out the lamps." The noise I heard was the crunching of snow under this man's feet. Some traveled on foot carrying a ladder and can of naphtha but the majority of them had a horse and cart. Well the city lamp man would turn off the naphtha lamps, fill up the little metal tank for the next evening's supply, clean the glass with his rag and pass on to the next lamp post and just before dark of the same day he would return and light the same lamp again for the ensuing night, but not with a modern match. He would use the old fashioned sulphur match which took several times as long to catch as our modern match of today. After a while the artificial gas was supplied to these lamp posts which eliminated the necessity of the lamp man carrying around the naphtha. That's the way Detroit was lighted in those days. That is the way Dr. Atterbury for many years saw his way around Detroit at night. Then after several years, followed the electric light towers to light the city. They reached to the heavens. Each one had an elevator in the center which took the daily attendant to the top to clean the glass and adjust the carbon. They were a great curiosity to all visitors to our city. Guests coming in on railway trains peered out of the coach windows miles away before they reached Detroit to get a first glimpse of these strange heavenly sights. But they had their day. They were so high that the foliage from the trees shut out a great part of their light. So they were discontinued and we have the present system of lighting.

JAMES THE COACHMAN AND THE OLD COACH DOG

How beautiful were the main thoroughfares of old Detroit, all double lined with towering shade trees now all gone by the industrial encroachment. Back of those trees were the spacious lawns in the midst of which stood the homes of the wealthy, designed by the best architects of the day and unexcelled in their beauty anywhere. Gone is this beautiful panorama never to return but the old folks will like to remember it and the young folks ought to know about it. And you old timers will remember James the coachman in uniform back in the 70's who drove his employer back and forth from the office and the rest of the family down to the center of the city to do their shopping. No electric cars in those days—only the old horse cars, no stoves in the car, only some straw on the floor of the car to keep your feet warm.

Do you remember the old spotted black and white coach dog under the coach? He followed the horse taking what seemed to be a precarious position under the body of the carriage. With mathematical precision he followed the horse's heels his nose pointing downward and only a few inches from the flying hoofs. If the horse quickened his gait so did the dog. If the horse slowed down so did the dog. Under all circumstances the distance between the horse's hoofs and the dog's nose remained about the same. It was a quaint sight, but it has left the scene forever. And then we cannot forget how the coachman left his stable and spacious grounds. Leaving he drove his equipage over an upwardly protruding elbow of gas pipe which opened the gate and after having passed through, he again drove his coach over a similarly upwardly protruding elbow which closed the carriage entrance to the grounds. This was all accomplished without the coachman leaving his seat.

We must not forget that Detroit gave to the nation Capt. Eber B. Ward, super financier of the entire northwest who made at Wyandotte in 1864 the first commercial Bessemer Steel and in 1865 the first steel rails made in America and who was the genesis of the United States Steel Corporation, out of whose genius finally sprang the laying of thousands of miles of railways, the manufacture of giant locomotives and great steel steamships, the building of towering sky-scrapers and eventually the manufacture of millions of automobiles and airplanes to make a mockery of time and space. Dr. Atterbury, Rev. Grandy and Capt. Ward all lived in the same day right here in Detroit.

Old Timers—Let us remember the millions of wild ducks and geese that flew right over our houses on their way south in the fall of the year. Long ago they deserted us. They don't like the big city life. Now they go around about us on their way south. And the pretty southern birds stay pretty much in the suburbs when they come north in the spring time. And the billions and billions of wild pigeons that used to blacken the sky in their flight right here in Detroit. What a tragedy. They're all gone forever. And Old Timers do you remember when you were a tiny little youngster a little island in the Detroit river called Hog Island and so known on all the maps by that name because it was infested with rattlesnakes and the owners of the island kept a herd of hogs on it to devour the snakes? Do you remember petitions being circulated around the city for your Dad to sign requesting the council to buy this Hog Island—drain it—convert it into a city park and name it Belle Isle? I do. Aren't we all glad today? It's a pretty good guess that Dr. Atterbury and Rev. Grandy both signed one of those petitions. It was about 1879.

THE HAMMOND BUILDING

Where the Hammond building now stands, before it was built, stood a white house. When the Hammond building was erected, it was considered such a colossal wonder that railway excursions were run into Detroit at lowered rates to see the great building. Some time between the years 1848 and 1853 the writer's father and mother lived in a little house next door to where the Hammond building now stands and kept a cow on the premises. I once heard my father telling some ladies about this and that he could have bought land at that time all around there for a song. One lady asked him why he didn't buy up a lot of it. His reply was that he didn't have the song.

And Old Timers, how many remember the cutter racing on Lafayette and Cass avenues? Detroit streets used to be all covered with snow all winter long. It was not a gambling proposition— just pure fun—one fellow's horse matched against another. First it was on Lafayette Avenue and then it was transferred to Cass Avenue. And do you remember hundreds of bob sleighs coming into town from the country loaded with dressed hogs on the way to Billy Perkin's Hotel on Grand River Avenue near Cass Avenue for the night so as to be on the central market on Cadillac Square bright and early next morning?

Do you remember the old central market on Cadillac Square many years ago torn down and is now the pony stable room at the head of Belle Isle rebuilt?

Do you remember Cadillac Square before it was paved, persons flitting from flag stone to flag stone, to escape sinking ankle deep into the mire?

Cadillac Square was filled with negroes who formed the Lime-kiln Club depicted many years ago by Mr. M. Quad of the Detroit Free Press. They did white washing and chimney sweeping and cut up your winter supply of cord wood at 50c per cord. The group while assembled there waiting for a customer discussed religion, politics or any subject that no one else was able to solve.

Across the road in front of the city hall stood a line of drays, the driver asleep on the seat waiting for a customer.

Looking south you saw G. & R. McMillan's fancy grocery establishment the swank spot where the carriage trade rolled up and the aristocracy of Jefferson Avenue bought their groceries and across the road the old Russell House where the Prince of Wales (later King Edward VII) made his speech. And looking in the opposite direction you saw Wright Kay & Co. store. On the roof was a large staff with a huge ball at the end of it. Each day at noon the ball would drop and people on the street would set their watch accordingly, 12 o'clock.

But folks these things have gone, never to return and Dr. Atterbury, Rev. Grandy and Dr. Barlow witnessed many of them. But Calvary Church still remains. And the Watson ordinance in full force only a few years ago which forbade any saloon or beer garden on Grand River Avenue this side of the Boulevard is no more. So Calvary Church with all the other forces for righteousness in this section must pool their assets to offer the youth something better than the beer garden has to offer.

ARCHITECT

Mr. Andrew R. Morrison was the architect of the Sutherland Memorial and has done a very creditable piece of work. We feel that our building is second to none.

CHRONOLOGICAL ORDER

Of events has not been strictly adhered to in writing this story of Calvary Church but the writer feels that he has given the reader most of the main facts in her history. However the scrap book in the safe is always available to any reader desiring more minute details on any particular phase of Calvary's History.

THE COMPLETED MEMORIAL

Was turned over to the pastor on Sunday, April 7th, 1940, as the picture shows but one glorious chapter remains.

V. C. PALMER   DR. LESLIE A. BECHTEL   DR. JOHN W. HOFFMAN
TURNING OVER KEYS TO SUTHERLAND MEMORIAL

CONSOLE OF GREAT CASARANT PIPE ORGAN
Installed in Calvary, 1943

THE NEW ORGAN

Above is shown the console. The pipes are all obscured. The organ cost originally $160,000 installed in Orchestra Hall. It would take seven freight cars to move it and weighs approximately 34,000 pounds. It was made by Casavant Bros. of St. Hyacinthe, Quebec, and originally donated to Orchestra Hall by Mr. and Mrs. William H. Murphy.

ONLY TWO LEFT

And over a period of 75 years there are only two persons left (still members of Calvary Church) whose parents were charter members and attended the Meat Market Mission on Michigan Ave., near 23rd street in 1868. They are Mrs. Wm. H. Blackford, daughter of Samuel Plumer on the first board of trustees and the writer's wife, Mrs. Wm. Downie Sr., daughter of David Reid, one of the first elders and a signer of the original articles of association.

WOMEN'S UNION

As there is no record of the officers of the Women's work, we do know that they were a tremendous help spiritually and financially in the up-building of the church including all kinds of charitable work, clothing, Christmas baskets to the needy, etc. After the church was started in its present location the women organized into two societies known as the Ladies' Aid and the Woman's Missionary Society. The Presidents were as follows:

LADIES' AID	WOMEN'S MISSIONARY
Mrs. F. Wescott	Mrs. D. I. Sutherland
Mrs. K. Kempton	Mrs. A. J. Marsh
Mrs. M. Coulton	Mrs. F. Clark
Mrs. Wm. Downie	Mrs. W. Newkirk

At the annual meeting, April 6, 1922, these two societies were united in one known as the Women's Union.

The Presidents were as follows to date:

Mrs. B. Thayer	Mrs. J. M. Hollinger
Mrs. N. J. Purinton	Mrs. A. Duncan
Mrs. Baker	Mrs. N. J. Thomas
Mrs. F. Woolfenden	Mrs. G. Wright
Mrs. J. Damman	Mrs. L. A. Bechtel
Mrs. J. Blair	Honorary President
Mrs. E. Bogen	

EVERYBODY INCLUDED

To the entire church school of religion, including Rev. MacElree, our choir, and splendid secretary, Mrs. Russell Armstrong,

Women's Union, the Junior Church, the Young People's C. E., the Jean Sutherland Guild, the Mother's Club, the Cleophas Club, the Hi-Club, Scout Troops 6 and 90, Girls Scout Troop 10, Cub Troop 6 Camp Fire Girls, the Horizon Club, Summer Vacation School and all religious activities of Calvary Church the latter extends her thanks for the splendid work you have all accomplished in the past years and here is hoping it may long continue. You've all done a good job, and we do not forget here Mr. Fred. A. McGregor, property custodian, whose aim is to please everybody.

A TRIBUTE TO THE OLD ORGAN

And to you, dear old organ, you've gone but we did not say goodbye without a touch of sadness. After forty years of service how could we? Coming along Grand River, on a Sunday morning, before even we crossed old Calvary's threshold, we've heard your glorious halleluiahs, proclaiming forth to Heaven your joyous message.

With tearful eyes we've listened to your mournful notes as our loved ones have been silently borne away. And with all the gaiety of youth we've heard "Here Comes The Bride" almost the last warning to two young lovers of the tremendous step they were about to take.

Ah, yes! dear old organ your job too has been well done and to you also, with voices a little husky, we again say good-bye and good-bye.

A PROPHECY MORE THAN FULFILLED

On Oct. 8th, 1916, ground was broken for the main church here at Grand River and Vicksburg Aves. Mr. Brinkerhoff, one of the old trustees, giving an address that day, said that he was going to prophesy that some day Calvary Church would be an organization of one thousand members. I doubt if many took the remark seriously because we were in pretty much of a wilderness at that time. But here we are with good able management, wise spending, keeping within our means, giving the community the very best of religious life, coupled with good social diversions. We have reached a church roll of about 1,700 with a standing for membership about third in the Detroit Presbytery. The entire unpaid balance on our church mortgage is about $6,700 with seven years to run at 4% interest. We have a Sunday school enrollment of about 800 and stand third or fourth in the Detroit Presbytery for membership. What a grand showing this is. Have our methods now not all been vindicated?

These splendid almost super-natural results since 1932 have been achieved under the masterful leadership of our beloved pastor, Dr. L. A. Bechtel, ably assisted by a retinue of determined, willing helpers many of whose names do not even appear in this history for lack of space so to them also we give due credit. But we cannot bring the story of Calvary to a close without furnishing roughly a list of her achievements in the last few years under Dr. Bechtel. These follow somewhat in detail and we here in conclusion wish to emphasize the valuable assistance in all church matters rendered by Mrs. Bechtel, his devoted wife, and the writer here expresses his sincere wish and knows that the congregation join him in wishing that Dr. and Mrs. Bechtel spend many, many more years in their highly successful work of both in Calvary Church.

AN ECONOMIC SUMMARY
"—something new has been added—"

In 12 years under Dr. Bechtel you have given in money, labor, time the following equipment to your Church:

300 copies of the Presbyterian Hymnal, Revised
400 hymnals for the Sunday School
250 Bibles for the Sunday School
50 gowns for the Adult Choir
50 gowns for the Intermediate Choir
75 gowns for the Junior Choir
Minister's robes and hood
Four office desks and three typewriters
Complete Multigraph Printing Equipment
Complete Automatic Offset Printing Equipment
Complete Addressograph Equipment
Intercommunication System through church
Filing cases, card index sets, 3 steel safes
Wardrobes, bookcases, cupboards for materials
16 mm Motion Picture Machine

Communion Equipment for 1,000 people
A well planned and beautiful stage with full electrical equipment
A large wardrobe of costumes and properties for pageants and dramatics
A Sunday School library of 500 volumes
A fairly adequate musical library for the choirs
A Church history and records, pictorial and literary, equalled by few churches in America
300 steel folding chairs for dining room
30 folding, hard wood tables for S. S. and church use
An illuminated outdoor bulletin board
A new water intake costing nearly $1,000
Storm windows for the colored glass costing $1,500

In capital construction and improvement you have:
Rebuilt the gymnasium to give 8 class rooms to the Junior S.S. and 100 more seats for the dining room
Rebuilt the kitchen at a cost of $2,000
Redecorated the Church Sanctuary twice
Constructed an educational building, completely furnished, at a cost of $68,000, of which only $6,750 remains to be paid.
Bought an organ which when installed, with necessary alterations, will cost in excess of $30,000.
Created a church estate of more than a quarter of a million dollars out of the original ground and buildings.
In addition you have paid all your bills 100 cents on the dollar, including bonds and mortgages.

       May the great work continue.
   How fleet the works of man,
   Back to their earth again,
   Ancient and holy things
   Fade like a dream.
                 Kingsley.

Calvary remains.
May, 1943.   **WILLIAM DOWNIE.**